About the Author

Holder of a Ph.D. from the Université de la Sorbonne (Paris IV) in American Civilization, Ahmed EL Hamzaoui has written *Transition to Democracy in Morocco* (2007), *An Investigation into Political Apathy Amongst Students* (2015), *Constitution-Building and Transitional Democracy in Morocco* (2016), *A Critical Discourse Analysis of some of Benkirane's Speeches* (2016), Moroccan *Women Standing at the Crossroads Between Modernity and Authenticity* (2017).

Sadij the Idiot

Ahmed El Hamzaoui

Sadij the Idiot

Olympia Publishers
London

www.olympiapublishers.com
OLYMPIA PAPERBACK EDITION

A CIP catalogue record for this title is
available from the British Library.

ISBN: 978-1-80074-297-0

This is a work of fiction.
Names, characters, places and incidents originate from the writer's
imagination. Any resemblance to actual persons, living or dead, is
purely coincidental.

First Published in 2023

Olympia Publishers
Tallis House
2 Tallis Street
London
EC4Y 0AB

Printed in Great Britain

Dedication

To my children: Imad, Zineb and Salma; without whom, this book wouldn't have seen the light of day.
To everybody who hates manipulative parents that attempt to establish psychological control over their children.

Acknowledgements

My special thanks of gratitude to my wife, Mouna, who has stuck with me through thick and thin.
My heartfelt appreciation also goes to my beloved sister, Touria, for her unfailing encouragement.

In loving memory of my dear mother
I wish I could be with you one last time, hear your soothing voice, and see your beaming smile. You are always in my heart but it's not the same.
I miss you dearly.

PART I

Chapter 1

Sadij, a five-year-old boy, was deeply engrossed in playing with his toys when he suddenly heard some moans emanating from the room adjoining his; he released hold of a red car his father had bought him for his birthday and made for the whereabouts of that peculiar whimper. To his dismay, he caught his mother, Makiera, in the act of embracing, kissing and caressing a stranger passionately in her bedroom. Upon discovering that his mum was engaged in sexual foreplay with a man other than his father, Sadij retraced his steps and dashed for his room. How would a little boy react when he found out that his mum was cheating on his father? The poor tyke was really in a quandary about which path to take.

'Do I tell? Do I hide it? Whose side do I take? And when my father finds out and my family is swept up in the ensuing emotional chaos, how do I hold it all together?'

The little boy kept asking himself, for he couldn't believe what he had seen, and it seemed as if his whole world had collapsed. How could a thoughtless mother impose her indiscretions on her offspring? How could a, so to speak, *good* mother have no awareness whatsoever of the huge damage that could be done to her child? In the throes of the chaos engendered by his mother's extramarital affair and the potential breakup that might ensue, Sadij was confused in his head, and couldn't think of anything else; he couldn't even resume trifling with his red car.

Meanwhile, on the landing, the good wife was seeing her lover off. *'Catch you later, dear one. I need to get back now.'* It seemed that the adulterous wife suffered no guilt, for she went back to her room singing as if she were rather entitled to the pleasure and excitement of her secret tryst; and at no time had it occurred to her to drop in and see what had become of her lonely son. Wasn't she getting what she needed in her marriage? In fact, in a breakup that had rocked her life, Makiera, who was twenty-seven, had split two weeks ago from her husband of four years, Taib, over her recurrent extramarital adventures. Instead of letting her kid know that she had slipped up with his father, she kept on telling him that he had gone on a trip.

The next day, Makiera picked up her son at school, bought him ice cream and took him home. When they went in, Sadij was stunned to see the same guy reposing on the couch watching TV. An excruciating feeling of resentment overtook the little boy, who declined his mother's command to greet the intruder, and scurried for his usual shelter. Makiera's face turned red with embarrassment, and she said to her lover, *'I'll be right back in a jiffy, Ablah.'* She scampered off into her son's room to have a word with him.

'What on earth do you think you're doing? Do you think this is the appropriate way to greet my friends? You have to mind your manners, my boy. Even if you don't relish the company of my friend, you've to make proof of good demeanour. Now, you had better apologise to him.'

'No way! I'm… not going to make an apology to… that guy,' stammered the poor little kid. *'Besides, I know him not and he has no right to be here while Dad is away from home.'*

Slighted, Makiera, beside herself with anger, started yelling at her son, *'Who are you to tell me what to do? Who is*

16

in charge here?' Feeling that the relational dance between her and her child was getting inverted, and being unable to resist the urge to rant and fume, she shouted out, *'As long as you're living under my roof, you'll do what I say.'*

Feeling his mother determined to put him down, diminishing him and kind of rubbishing him in front of a stranger, Sadij grabbed his favourite toy and hurled it at his mum. Instead of giving her child a good dressing-down, she started spanking him to assert her authority. This corporal punishment didn't make Sadij averse to bad behaviour. He just got angrier and started saying, *'Why should I do what you're telling me just because you're beating me?'*

Makiera didn't know that no beating and no threat of violence was going to work, for Sadij continued throwing a tantrum and banging his fist on the ground till the blood trickled down onto the floor. In place of exploring deterring strategies with her kid, such as removal of some privileges granted to him, she resorted to physical punishment.

In the living room, Ablah could hear the ongoing tumult, but couldn't and had no right to stop it; a few minutes later, Makiera joined him and he asked her what was going on, to which she answered, *'Well, you know when kids get into a fit of anger over paltry things… oh! Forget about it. Do you have any plans for tomorrow?*

'Nothing special, but if you want, we can have lunch in that Chinese restaurant I told you about last time.'

'To be honest, let's put it off until next week because I feel jaded. I have been doing a lot of overtime lately to save for a vacation.'

'Never mind, you'll be my guest and I'm inviting you for dinner tomorrow night. Right?'

'All right, darling!' The lovers kissed goodbye.

Chapter 2

Telling her child that she was dating someone else other than his father was a daunting challenge for Makiera. The latter was sitting by herself musing over the incident that transpired yesterday. *How can I tell him what made his father go south? Just wondering how my child can deal with the fact that there can possibly be another man in my life? How do I tell my child that I have begun a romantic relationship with someone new, someone he couldn't bear the sight of yesterday? I guess I need to broach this topic with him, come what may.*

Meanwhile, Sadij shut himself in his bedroom refusing to even see his mother, whom he thought was kind of betraying his father. What an emotional fall-out this infidelity might have on the little child, no one could tell. The emotional stress that would certainly follow from this incident would undoubtedly create serious scars that might never heal. How could a 'caring' mother put her sexual flings above the needs of her only child? Wasn't she supposed to be tuned in to her child's needs? Didn't she know that for her kid to thrive, she ought to attend to his pressing needs? Sadij was too young to understand what was happening and the whole world around him seemed to fall apart. He was too young to understand what was going on. It was as if he were born to suffer; at that very moment, he wished he were never born.

'How I wish my dad were here! I still find it hard to trust

my mother when she tells me that my dad is traveling and that he'll be back very soon.'

All of a sudden, Sadij's thoughts were interrupted by a voice that seemed familiar to him; it was his mother calling him for lunch. But he was in a sulk and in no mood to talk; he displayed a sullen aloofness and withdrawal. Yet, the voice kept on calling and Sadij turned a deaf ear to it. Tired of waiting for an answer that would probably never come, Makiera headed towards her son's room in the hope of making up with him.

'Come on, dearest one, you're not going to have the hump for the rest of the day. I'm sorry I shouted at you, but I didn't know what else to do because you wouldn't listen to me and you... and when you...'

Upon hearing this contradictory and seemingly conciliatory message, the little boy felt blamed and threatened, which made the whole attempt at ironing out the differences between mother and son futile. It appeared that his mother hadn't reached the feeling of wanting to repair yet; she couldn't find another more efficient way to offload her resentment. As a 'caring' mother, she didn't know how to release the emotional charge in a healthy way.

She then went on to say, *'I can see that you're still upset; you don't have to say sorry if you're still upset. What do you need to come back to peace? Do you want me to kneel to beg you for forgiveness?'*

Seeing that his mum's eyes were filled with tears, the little urchin felt empathy and said, *'I'm sorry for what I've done...'*

To which, the mother unexpectedly responded, *'Sorry is an easy word to say and there's no point in saying sorry if you're going to do that again.'*

It was as if she were once again not aiming to make her way back to genuine peace with her child.

'Go along with you and don't expect me to accept a stranger to be part of my life. You think that beating me will make me do what you want?' He began sobbing and kept on taking his mum to task for having hit him so violently. *'You hit me because my father is not around to protect me and I'm weaker and smaller than you!'*

Trying to restore the connection with her child, she awkwardly said, *'Oh, my little cute son. I'm sorry I spanked you; you know I love you very much, let's have a hug and make it up.'*

Sadij remained silent and couldn't bear looking his mum in the eyes.

'Come on, sweetheart, you know I love you, but I've just lost my temper. Just tell me what do I have to do to make it up to you.'

To get back in sync with her child, Makiera invited Sadij to play his favourite Super Mario game, challenging him by saying, *'I'll beat you this time. Ready to take up the challenge, dear one?'*

Finally, Sadij responded to play and things seemed to get better.

Chapter 3

As Sadij came out of school, he was joyfully surprised to find his grandmother waiting to pick him up. It was customary for Moukafiha to bring her grandson home from school, as his mother was getting inured to it. Makiera was lucky enough to have her child's grandparents living nearby and was then availing herself of what she believed was a godsend to use them for her child care. But that was not for occasional babysitting as normal mothers do, but it was for full-time care while she was having fun or casual sexual relationship with one of her lovers. When the little kid caught sight of his beloved grandmother, he went into raptures and hurried off to throw himself in her arms. He knew in his own heart of hearts that she loved him and cared for him and would take care of him to the very best of her abilities. The need to care and protect Sadij overtook any angry feelings she had for her callous daughter.

'My little one, come and snuggle in my arms.'

Her grandchild was delightful and loved as much as she loved her children. She did a lot of the child care and babysitting; she didn't envisage doing this in her fifties but felt strongly that she had to support her daughter. Therefore, she had given up most of her spare time to do this. She knew that her daughter was very immature, rude and any attempt to discuss anything or to bring her to reason would unmistakably trigger a negative reaction. She had repeatedly explained to her daughter that she should stop having her lovers over lest her infidelity should have a lasting and negative impact on Sadij. Mrs Moukafiha was shouted down every time she wanted to reason her daughter out of her dissolute disposition.

The caring grandmother took the little boy to California Bliss in Champigny-sur-Marne to taste frozen yogurts, a Californian specialty that Sadij liked so much. Mrs Moukafiha's unfailing presence in the boy's life provided stability, support and nurture, for she had turned out to be a buffer during these times of family distress. She did not only meet the emotional need of the boy, but she also provided financial assistance whenever the need arose.

'Can you show me something you learned or did today?' asked the grandmother.

'Yeah,' replied the boy. *'We did some mathematical operations, especially addition and subtraction.'*

'Did you get on well with them?'

'A piece of cake. I did all math exercises with success.'

'I'm proud of you, smart lad,' said the grandma, expressing great joy.

'Did any of your classmates do anything funny?'

Sadij didn't reply straightaway, for he was enjoying his special and delicious ice cream; realising that it took him a while to respond to his grandma's question, Sadij answered quickly, *'Sure, sure, indeed; something very funny happened. Someone knocked on the door during class and one of my classmates got the whole class to freak out and yelled that we were under attack and all of us did hide under the desks. But the man that rapped at the door turned out to be no one else but the school principal.'*

'Oh! That's funny. Tell me, dear one, did the teacher give you some homework to do?'

'No, not this time, he rather told us to do an Internet search for Joan of Arc and the Hundred Years' War,' replied the boy with great alacrity.

Mrs Moukafiha took a glance at her watch and said, 'Look at the time, it's getting late. Let's do like a banana and split!'

The two made their way through the squalid quarters and filthy slums of Champigny-sur-Marne. Living in the suburbs was just like living in precariousness. Well-advised parents living in the suburbs of Paris had no other choice but to keep their offspring on a leash, and not leave them at the bottom of an old block of flats lest they might mingle with some ruffians loitering and standing in passers-by's way.

From the end of the nineteenth century until 1970, there was in France a great housing crisis. The French State decided to build on the outskirts of cities, large buildings grouped into districts. These low-income suburban dwellings were initially made for people or families who had modest financial resources. Unfortunately, some French suburbs had become hot spots for a serious crime (drug, cars and weapons trafficking, cargo thefts, armed robberies); these marginalised suburbs turned into strongholds of delinquency. Moukafiha, a very sensitive and sacrificial woman, had all the time been worried sick about her children's future. She, unlike her husband, Bakhil, had always thought that this great concern for kids was part of being a parent and made sense; deep down, she had always believed that that concern and care for the well-being of her children had unfailingly enabled her to set limits and keep her children safe and on the right track.

Nevertheless, it dawned upon her that such excessive worries just didn't make sense, especially when such anxious parenting didn't work out with all her children. While Sadij was watching TV, Mrs Moukafiha started musing.

That little child's whole future would be in jeopardy if I weren't here. He would be unmotivated, disrespectful and wouldn't be able to make friends. I doubt how he would fare in adulthood.

She began thinking about the future and having a negative view of what the future would hold in store for Sadij if she weren't close by. Fortunately, she knew that this pattern of negative thinking didn't tally with reality, for Sadij was a little mature boy that was too much ahead of his time.

Bringing up a child in a disadvantaged neighbourhood was a daunting challenge for a divorced woman, and Mrs Moukafiha held a grudge against her daughter, who didn't care a hang about her child. The grandma sometimes felt there was no future for her grandson in that damned Square Carpeaux; every day, when she went down to get some French baguettes and milk, there were often some young commuters or *banlieusards* hanging around in the corners of the street, screaming and shouting, others waiting to quarrel and wrangle. So, she didn't like the way the children were being brought up in close vicinity and kept on laying the blame both on careless and indifferent parents and the French government that placed immigrants on the periphery of society by creating ghettos.

Moukafiha's brooding was distracted by a phone call and that was Makiera, who 'inquired after' her child.

'Hello, Ma. Is he still awake?'

'Tell me first when will you be home?' asked Mrs Moukafiha.

'Not yet, but I don't think I'll come home before eleven p.m.'

That was the last straw and Mrs Moukafiha sounded off about this unbearable and unseemly behaviour of her daughter.

'What? Are you kidding me? If you think I should keep

looking after your child while you pursue a single lifestyle, then let me tell you that you're dead wrong.'

Mrs Moukafiha felt put upon; she cared for the little kid, but couldn't help feeling resentful of her daughter's unfettered lifestyle. Besides, she had had enough of trying to conceal that scandalous behaviour of her daughter from her husband. She, for the first time, told her daughter a few home truths, *'Listen! It's a blessing to have a grandchild around, but I didn't retire just to be a baby sitter. I decided to help you out, but in no way am I going to raise your child. I already reared six children.'*

'Cut the crap!' impudently replied Makiera, who begged Ablah's permission and moved a few steps away to speak comfortably. *'You ain't gonna stop me from living my life. You ain't the one to prevent me from getting out there and doing what I like.'*

Mrs Moukafiha tried to pull herself together, but she was beside herself with anger, and lashed out at her daughter, *'Put a sock in it, you fatuous girl. The bottom line is that this needs to be stopped! Don't ever expect me to pick up your son from school every weekday afternoon.'*

Mrs Moukafiha wanted to remind her daughter of her duties as a mother, outright refusing to sit in the first place. Refusing to pick up Sadij from school had nothing to do with the love she cherished in her innermost heart for the boy; she just felt like she paid her dues, for she once was a stay-at-home mother, and never had any outside help or caring for her brood.

'You think you're entitled to everything, and we, your parents, should babysit for your child whether we want to or not while you're having fun with those scoundrels of yours. Let me set you straight on this. From now on, you will have to take your full responsibility as a mother. Dig?'

Then she put the phone down on Makiera. Listlessly,

shoulders drooping, she entered her bedroom muttering to herself, *'I'm on call every day. I don't say anything because he is my grandchild, but she needs to know that it is her duty as a mother to raise her child and attend to his needs.'*

While deeply engrossed in her thoughts, Mrs Moukafiha's interior monologue was abruptly interrupted by her husband's question, *'What on earth are you muttering to yourself? Are you off your chump?'*

'I was just thinking about... Oh, forget it!' She was about to blurt it out, but eventually regained her composure, for she knew that if she ever broached the subject of her daughter's irresponsibility towards her child, she would certainly ignite Bakhil's petulance, as he was a very irascible man, who was inured to outbursts of temper, whenever he felt the tranquil and cosy life he was leading threatened.

Bakhil was a lazy guy who spent most of his time sprawled out on the couch, eyes glued to Canal+ and at no time during his married life had he done the dishes, taken out the trash, cleaned up after meals, or lent a helping hand to his wife. He got into the habit of leaving a mess behind without considering the hectic workload shouldered by his wife. The latter was the one who usually did the household chores. Besides, she was the one to support the whole family with her earnings, while the fainéant was on the dole, not because there was no work to do, but because within the bloke there was that morbid disinclination to activity and exertion despite possessing the capacity to exert himself.

Chapter 4

The next day, Mrs Moukafiha took the child to school because his mum was still in the arms of Morpheus as a result of her having taken part in a licentious revelry. Notwithstanding Makiera's casual sexual relations with different partners, her mother tried with all her might to enhance her communication and connection with her daughter, cutting down on clashes, but to no avail.

The primary complaint that Makiera had about her mum was that she tried to parent her and was overly critical and demanding. For Mrs Moukafiha, the only way to improve her relationship with her daughter was for the latter to change her ways. Before Makiera got married five years ago, Mrs Moukafiha had had idealistic expectations about her. Shortly after having tied the knot, she engaged in illicit dalliances with some young teenagers in the neighbourhood.

The whole mess began when Taib, Makiera's former husband, travelled to Morocco to see his family; all this while, Taib would give her buzz and ask after her and their only child, and Makiera would behave as if she were a pious lady left on her own in a whole wild world. But the truth came out when back in France, one day the couple had a scuffle, and Makiera left home and went to live with her parents. A few days later, Taib spotted her wandering around with a young sturdy *banlieusard*. When he confronted her, she immediately denied the accusation and said that he was just a friend of her brother's. He then patched up things with her and convinced her to return home. But very soon, she made friends with another old man that turned out to be Taib's close friend.

The first time that Taib got a sneaking feeling that his wife was cheating on him was one day when her family was throwing a party to celebrate the birth of a new born baby girl, Taib caught Makiera in the act of looking into the eyes of her cousin for a long time, playing with her hair, wrapping a hair strand around her finger, caressing it, and biting her lower lip. Taib couldn't bring himself to accept to be a cuckold, for he hailed from a very conservative Muslim family where such indecorous gestures were morally inappropriate. He was devastated and didn't know what to do. Since he had to fend for his child and had no intention of forsaking him, Taib thought that divorce was not an option; rather than taking a permanent and rash decision, he time and time again sat her down and asked her what she wanted, if she wanted anything, but in vain. Eventually, he felt his relationship was gone and didn't feel like looking at her. All the time, the pictures of those guys came to haunt him.

The immediate days and weeks following the realisation that his wife was a nymphomaniac were full of extremely strong emotions that wavered between disgust and bitterness; after learning that he had been deceived and betrayed, something deep inside of him was touched – it eradicated the belief in the woman whom he had been loving all along, it destroyed the belief in himself and caused him to call into question all that he had believed about his marriage so far. He would often wonder how he could have been such a naive dolt to have trusted an unfaithful woman, and the shame of having been put upon deepened his injury; passing by the places he and his wife had been to was just like rubbing salt into his wounds. He would spend hours and hours turning in on himself and eating his heart out. Every time he tried to give their marriage a second chance, every moment he attempted to speak to her, to have a very open and honest conversation, she turned it into an argument, and was not remorseful. Every endeavour to repair his marriage, to heal the pain and rebuild trust had fallen through.

At no time had she accepted responsibility for being unfaithful; she had never understood the hurt she had caused or at least brought herself to apologise. But what actually exasperated Sadij was the fact that Makiera still wouldn't confess to having stabbed him in the back several times; he knew beyond a shadow of a doubt that she had cheated on him, but she refused to admit it, and at times downplayed the details. The real truth was that what made Taib pack up his suitcase and leave the whole relationship was not just an affair, it was the frequency with which she had broken his frail heart, thus establishing a pattern of behaviour he could not put up with.

At one time, he tried to just get used to the facts that had been laid bare, started to adjust and trust again, and then as the French saying goes, 'When what is natural is driven off, it returns at a gallop'. Therefore, the betrayed poor chap gave up trying to pick up the pieces, and seeing that his wife continued to be selfish, shady and untrustworthy, withholding information and doing things behind his back, he decided to end his marriage. In the wake of this emotional betrayal in marriage, Taib concluded that there were no authentic personal relationships and that the exchange of wedding vows was all lies and jest.

Chapter 5

When Sadij turned seven years old, he started hitting his mother; he would throw things whenever he got indignant, and one time he grabbed an ashtray from a table and hurled it at her. Sometimes, parental abuse might take the shape of verbal abuse, and this was what Sadij once did when he started calling her names and treating her like a slut on account of seeing her have it off with some guys she had introduced to him as friends.

Her parental authority and credibility had been severely damaged in the aftermath of her divorce from Taib. Sadij started showing far less respect towards his mother; he listened less and gave her grief about everything she might ask him to do. The young man looked at his mother as being responsible for the departure of his father, for she was the one who had broken wedding vows. He realised that his mother's talk about things like integrity, honesty, responsibility, kindness et cetera was all humbug in that her actions did not match her words.

One day, while taking him for a ride, Makiera tried to warn her son against hanging out with a boisterous friend of his.

Sadij got greatly incensed. '*You cheated Dad. You've been skirting your duties towards me as a mother, and now you're talking to me about how to choose a good friend?*'

Makiera felt trapped as if she were in a car without brakes, and couldn't take action. She pulled the car up at the curb, took out her cell phone to call Taib to come to her rescue.

'Hello, Taib. How's it going?'

'I'm fine, thanks. How's Sadij doing?' he inquired.

'Actually, he's driving me crazy at the moment, and his behaviour is bordering on being abusive.'

Meanwhile, the young man at the back of the car released the car seat buckle and wriggled out of his belt in an attempt to snatch the phone from his mother, who said to Taib, *'Well, here's Sadij. He wants to talk to you.'*

'Hello, Pa. I missed you so much. You know, Mother is so unkind to me, and there's a man she keeps going out with all the time... he often comes home, his name is Ablah.'

Upon hearing this, Makiera brutally took the phone away from her son and tried to digress, but in vain, for Taib started rebuking her for having let a stranger come into his son's life. *'How dare you to introduce my son to a stranger? It's shameful. Do you want your child to believe that you're a scarlet woman?'*

'Come on, slow your roll, fool. You're just imagining things as usual. Well, it's no use talking to you. You'll always remain a diehard primitive man. I guess I've got to keep a lid on this call 'cause you're going too far.'

Chapter 6

A man never has the family he wants. Too normal or too crazy, torn or stuffy… Whatever family we come from, there is always something to complain about. But it is by trying to do better that we build our happiness. Is anyone ever satisfied with their lot? I think not, because if we had the ideal family, we wouldn't want to start one. It stands to reason that there are childhoods from which we recover less well than others. Some may grumble, 'We don't choose our parents. We don't choose our family.' But generally speaking, any individual always has good reasons to complain about his own. The family is a space of fantastical construction in which we try to forge an identity, between the family that we believe we had and the one that we would have liked to have, between idealised representations and inevitably disappointing reality.

As the years went by, Sadij knew in his heart of hearts that many people in this life did struggle with complex family dynamics. The only thing he knew for sure was that his father had never had the intention of walking out on him as his mother would lash out at him whenever he refused to comply with her preposterous injunctions. However, the constant bleak picture that she kept drawing about his father had stirred something in him and made him feel unwarranted rancour towards his father. Indeed, Makiera had managed to ascribe her failed marriage to Taib. That was the last straw for Sadij, who had not spoken to his father for the last ten years. He could not bring himself to forgive his father for the childhood emotional trauma he had inflicted.

For Sadij, now seventeen, the road to forgiveness seemed to be too long and too irksome, and there seemed to be no light at the end of the tunnel. Sadij had on several occasions the opportunity to see that his mother was not as perfect as he thought. But she at least, or so he thought, stood by him and fended him off while Taib was thousands of miles away from him. At times when Makiera took him to task for petty things, he would then begin to imagine that his parents were not his parents, that he must have been kidnapped, snatched from a more loving and more understanding couple. Who knew?

The family is the object of a strong idealisation, as we project onto it our need for security and kindness, and we find it hard to accept that it could be something other than a cocoon. When Sadij was all by himself, he would often talk ruefully to himself about the absence of his father and the recklessness and dissoluteness of his mother, thus imagining that he was doomed to a complicated fate.

'Why does this happen to me? What did I do to deserve such an ominous fate?'

Nevertheless, Sadij was not yet in a position to digest the notion that the divorce of his parents was the upshot of psychic and emotional failure, and that the latter could have led to violence, were it not for that marital break-up; hence, that separation was a blessing in disguise in that it did relieve his parents of insoluble conflicts and eased tensions. But what lacerated Sadij's feelings was those embarrassing moments when the teacher would ask to see his father; he didn't know what to say. Sometimes, he would take a roundabout path to avoid a neighbour who would ask after his father. He found it really hard to utter the truth that his father was gone and perchance for good. Lest he should experience that feeling of embarrassment and shame, he would say to those who took delight in prying into his affairs that his father had died in a car accident.

Sadij was at this specific period of puberty, going through physical and emotional changes that brought him an increasingly sexual and gender awareness, and unavoidable physical and mental blossoming. The turnaround involved changes in Sadij's relationship with his grandma, for he was expected now to get himself to school and be responsible for budgeting his own time. This came at a time when he began questioning the authority of his mother and other adults in his life. At this crucial moment, while pushing back the boundaries, he was desperately in need of an adult to guide him and set limits to his potential deviations from moral standards.

A positive mother-child relationship could have been a protective factor that might atone for the absence of Sadij's father and spare the young man the risks of developing behavioural disorders. However, Sadij turned out to be a very stoic young man who was poignantly aware of the challenges at stake and made up his mind to face them boldly and not capitulate; he devoted his time to study.

Now that Makiera had decided to get married to Ablah, Sadij contrived a plan; he wanted to make it, against all odds. He was well-cognisant of the fact that he had to move heaven and earth in an attempt to ward off academic failure, and the fear of engaging in delinquency got more and more intense, thus inducing the young man to give his time, his attention and self to study.

At first, Sadij didn't have any math textbooks, and therefore he got them issued from the school library. He did the same for English and science. He would remain awake past his usual bedtime studying math and science and before turning in, he would dabble at some English oral communication. He was resolute to fend for himself without asking for any assistance from anyone else.

His primary concern was to put away some money to purchase some other books that would help him in other subjects; hence, on weekends, he decided to give a helping hand to a Moroccan grocer in the vicinity in exchange for a petty sum of money that was to become his pocket money. His work consisted in replenishing the stock on the store shelves and helped customers find items they might be looking for. With the small allowance he earned, he could somctimes go to the cinema, or afford to eat at McDonald's as his peers weren't able to do.

Sometimes, he would bring his books with him to the store and leaf through them. One day, the owner of the grocery undertook a short trip to place an order for the purchase of some foodstuffs and other various household supplies he had run out of. When he returned to his store, and very much to his amazement, he found Sadij sprawling out his books on the counter and deeply engrossed in conning some math formulae. The moment the owner walked in, Sadij sprang to his feet. He knew he was up to something bad, for he was — if there were no customers around — supposed to be cleaning the store and replenishing the grocery shelves when items went out of stock, for there was always something to do, as the boss usually kept saying.

Mr Bakkal, that was the name of the owner of the grocery, was beside himself with anger; he started rebuking Sadij for having shirked his assigned responsibilities.

'Where do you think you are? You've been sitting here for goodness knows how long twiddling your thumbs. You're here to toil and the money you earn should be deserved! You dig, young lazy lad?'

Sadij remained speechless, staring open-mouthed, and with great difficulty, he, at last, managed to apologise to his boss. *'I'm so sorry, sir. I promise I'll never do that again. You have my word of honour'*

The sturdy chap issued a warning, *'Well, I'm willing to wipe the slate clean this time, and give you a fresh start. But in the event of a repeat offense, I will give you the boot. Do you understand?*

'Yea, sir,' replied the young man in a very low, bashful voice.

Chapter 7

Makiera needed a man to take care of her and her son, Sadij; so, she got married. After Taib and Makiera had split up, Ablah became a never-ending fixture in Sadij's life, turning up every day to drive him to school and back. Sadij could barely put up with his arrogance, for the latter showed contempt for the have-nots; whenever Ablah drove Sadij to school, Sadij would sit in the farthest corner of his sumptuous sport Golf car. Sadij could recollect that his father Taib had never owned a luxury car, but Sadij would have walked with his father to school rather than have a ride in a very expensive car with a man who thought he was the cat's whiskers. Sadij's life turned into a real nightmare the day his mother married Ablah. He could remember his mother was very ecstatic, and the soothing words she had said to him at the time kept coming back.

'You will see. We will be just fine!' Unfortunately, Sadij ended up paying the price for his mother's happiness.

Sadij could remember that his stepfather was a very nice bloke at first, for he would buy him gifts and would take him to fast-food restaurants. Then, things had changed for the worse when his younger brother was born, and everything went haywire. He would treat him as a slave. One day, after his return from work, he lay on the couch and indolently asked Sadij to perform some foot massages in the presence of Makiera.

'You know, honey, I've been working like a dog, and those dexterous hands of Sadij are just kind of pain relief; this makes me feel so good and alleviates stress.'

'Of course, darling. Sadij likes you so much and is ready to do whatever you want,' said Makiera in a very reassuring voice.

Sadij, who was rubbing Ablah's foot all over, holding the top of each foot with both hands and using small circular motions with his thumbs on each toe, couldn't prevent his mother from savouring that bogus matrimonial bliss, though Ablah's feet did stink. Sometimes, when Makiera was away from home working in a nearby hospital as a student nurse, Ablah would order Sadij to clean the floor or wash the dishes. At times, he would ask him to change his younger brother's diaper. He would threaten to spank him if he ever refused to comply with his commands. What irked Sadij was that Ablah used to ascribe his ill-treatment of Sadij to the fact that he wasn't his real father.

A few years later when Sadij got a bit bigger, things changed and he could no longer let his stepfather walk all over him. One day, Sadij and one of his classmates were going over and seriously restudying some algebra classroom material for a final exam when suddenly appeared from nowhere his stepfather, who superciliously ordered him to wash his car. Sadij got pissed off because he couldn't bear being humiliated before his friend; he then decided to take the piss out of his stepfather by retorting, 'Does it look like it's written on my forehead that I'm a car detailer?'

From that day on, Ablah and Sadij started ignoring each other and scarcely said hello to each other whenever they bumped into each other. In no time, they developed an aversion towards each other. When conflicts broke out, Makiera would take up the cudgels for her husband, even if she knew for sure that he had been acting unfairly towards her child. Whenever a bone of contention skidded, she would side with her husband and lay all the blame on her son. As time went by, Makiera and her husband started behaving differently towards Sadij. Accordingly, the young man felt rejected and unwanted. She even stopped talking to her son for more than a week.

Sadij was all by himself, with no one to turn to confide in. He lay in his bed mulling over what went wrong. *I didn't even do anything to her. Why is she always defending him? I used to find excuses for her blatant mistakes, but now that she is letting me down, I have had scales fall from my eyes, and I can see how selfish and narcissistic she is. What a fool I have been to fail to realise she has always treated me with disregard and has never given a damn about me. Actually, and right after my dad had left, she had known several guys. She would always be in cahoots with one of them and gang up on me. I have to get out of their lives as soon as possible.*

Chapter 8

Before and even after Makiera got married, she had been fostering and nurturing to grow Sadij's rejection of his father, and she had been doing it to bolster her identity. She had been manipulating Sadij for many years to abhor his father, making her child by hook or by crook believe that his father had of his own free accord walked out on him, despite Sadij's unshakable conviction that she was the only one who screwed up his family's life. Instead of providing her son with truly unconditional motherly love, she had been ruthlessly withholding the love her little child was desperately and innately in need of. All her manoeuvres were designed to denigrate Taib, who took a lot of flak for something he didn't do.

Once she came home very late and drunk, bringing with her someone whom she called her night work buddy. But when Sadij had tried to set limits to her blatant debauchery, she guilt-tripped him, whimpering, *'You just don't know what it feels like for a woman to be by herself and to have to meet the basic needs of a child. Besides, who is going to pay the gas, electricity and water bills?'* She immediately jumped into her victim role and started disparaging his father. *'Let me set the record straight once and for all. Who wears the pants in here? Let me remind you in case you've forgotten that your father doesn't send any alimony to provide for your needs.'*

Makiera's main aim was to blemish the reputation and the image of her former husband in her son's mind; she had been creating an expectation that her child chooses sides all the while. So, Sadij had been manipulated by her to more than hate Taib, despite all evidence to the contrary. How could a sane mother engage in programming her child to denigrate his father? She even went so far as to strike fear into Sadij's heart when she wanted her child to never go with his father if the latter ever came to pick him up from school.

'You have to be more suspicious when it comes to talking to strangers. You have to fear strangers because some of them may turn out to be predators; they may kidnap you and maltreat you.' How could a caring mother draw such a nightmare scenario to a little child?

Upon hearing this, Sadij started freaking out, but all of a sudden, he pulled himself together in an effort not to appear as a craven boy. He then said to his mother, *'How capable is my father really of hurting me, his son?'*

'Well, I'm just warning you, that's all. Besides, your father wants to take you away from me; he is determined to take you to Morocco.'

Makiera had never been concerned about her son; she was merely adamant about doing whatever she could to undermine and meddle with Sadij's relationship with his father, and that was a patent token of her inability to break free from the impact of her divorce and focus on the pressing needs of Sadij. Such on-ongoing denigration and constant badmouthing had unfortunately led to Sadij's emotional rejection of Taib. Worse than that, the divorce of his parents had instilled in him a fear of abandonment concerning all of his relationships. He became fraught with mistrust, for he started believing that when things went wrong, he would be forsaken. At school, he lacked a knack for evening out differences with his peers.

Sadij knew in his heart of hearts that his campaign of casting aspersions on his father had no justifications; however, he couldn't bring himself to admit that it was the outcome of his mother's indoctrination and brainwashing. His views of his father, Taib, were virtually and exclusively so negative that his father was demonised and seen as evil. The parental alienation Makiera had been engaged in involved an array of strategies she made use of to belittle and vilify Taib to her son. That emotional child abuse that she had been performing included badmouthing, in which she took delight even in the presence of her lover. One day, Sadij had refused to do Ablah a favour, which pushed Makiera to freak and lose the noodle, ranting against what she qualified as ungratefulness on the part of her son.

'You know what they say; like father, like son. You just look like him; a weak, selfish and two-faced pathological liar.'

Makiera's hatred of her former husband knew no bounds, for each time Taib attempted to establish contact with his son, Makiera would hang up on him, making contact with his son impossible, even worse erasing Taib from the life and mind of her son. While leafing through her son's copybooks, she came across a picture of Taib that Sadij kept all the time for himself, and tore it up into pieces.

When Sadij discovered that the picture had gone missing, he asked his mother, *'Hey, Ma! Have you by any chance seen a picture I laid into my English book?'*

Playing the innocent, Makiera abruptly answered, *'What picture are you talking about? Do you think that there's nothing I can do except rummaging through your personal*

42

belongings? Are you nuts?'

To avoid getting into any confrontation with his mother, he didn't want to insist any more. So, he put his books away in his satchel and hurried off to school.

Makiera, more out of rancour than out of love, used every means available to coerce her child into rejecting his father, presenting to the mind of her then little child a very bleak picture of his dad, forcing Sadij at times to choose between either living with her in compliance with her terms or going to Morocco and live with the poor extended family of his father. Her unmotherly lunacy had impelled her one day to threaten her child with withdrawing affection. There were times when she would give her little child the cold shoulder for days at a stretch. Makiera used emotional retribution and appeared to be unaware of the harmful impact that this could have on Sadij. The poor little urchin was emotionally insecure and attention-seeking.

One day while discussing the matter with one of her sisters, Makiera took the lid off the fact that Sadij kept reminding her of her ex-husband.

'The things he does, the way he talks and walks. I mean his dad still lives with us.'

'You had better start a new life and leave the past behind if you wish to be happy,' said Moutalaiba, advising her elder sister.

'You know, sister, I've decided to remain staunchly steadfast in my relationship with Ablah. He is broad-minded, doesn't give a hang about religious norms, easy-going and altogether outgoing.'

'So, you've already taken the first steps to get to know each other. If I were you, I would create new memories to

replace the old ones,' said Moutalaiba, encouraging her sister to turn over a new page, and move forward.

'But how can I make Sadij love and accept Ablah as a stepfather?' cried out Makiera, wrinkling her brow and drawing down the corners of her mouth.

'Let me just put this straight, you can't expect a deep bond to develop between your child and Ablah overnight. Just try to help Sadij adjust to the new situation and encourage him to give Ablah a chance.'

'Trust me, I've tried so many times, but it just doesn't work. He really loves his father and cannot get him off his mind. But I guess I need to have someone to provide for both of us, and that he should be aware of.' She cast a glance at her wrist-watch and said, *'Oh! it's getting late, I have to boogie. So long, dear sister. Catch you later.'*

'Take care and remember my advice,' said Moutalaiba, following her sister down the stairs that led to the elevator.

Chapter 9

Meanwhile, Makiera out of rancour kept intercepting all the letters that Taib had sent to his son, Sadij. In one of those letters, Taib wrote:

Dear son,
You just can't imagine how much I love you. Believe me, I have never meant to hurt you; you mean so much to me. I know that a father's role in a son's life is so crucial. Although the dynamics between the two of us are almost non-existent, I do know that my involvement as a father in your life can surely have a significant impact on the development of your masculine identity and will, and in a way, shape the kind of man you will become later. How I wish I could right now be by your side, cook for you, drop you off at school, pick you up and even read your stories before you go to bed. In a word, the only burning desire I have is to spend more time with you. This is my fifth letter to you. I was expecting you to answer just one of them. Every day, I check my pillar-box hoping to find a letter, and whenever the postman passes by, a flicker of hope is rekindled in me. I hope, dear son, that you hold no grudge against me. Remember, my son, I will always approve of anything you may undertake to build your self-esteem so that you can face the outside world with confidence and fulfilment. You need to know that your father is proud of who you are and

of the man you will become. It is for this reason that both of us need to develop intimate ties through exchanging letters because whenever I try to contact you by phone, your mum keeps hanging up on me.

Always on my mind and down deep in my soul,
Dearest and only son,
Your loving father,
Taib, whose main concern is your happiness.

Taib was, against his will, deprived of the opportunity to guide and set his son on the right path because of his unfaithful wife. He could have managed to move his way out of it, but he couldn't get over it. He was upset, betrayed and let down; he started calling into question his self-worth. The more he attempted to overlook these painful emotions, the longer they lingered.

At first, he tried to put on a brave face and act as if nothing did happen, but it didn't work out. He tried to live a normal life, but Makiera's unceasing flings did leave him with no choice. When he was cheated on, Taib kept reproaching himself; *Wasn't I enough? Wasn't I able to make her feel good?* He unfortunately never received an accurate answer because Makiera was a lecherous nymphomaniac.

Taib, a cultured and well-educated man, knew in his own heart of hearts that his absence in the life of his son would inevitably lead to certain character disorders such as instability, anger and excessive emotionality. To avenge herself against Taib for having thrown his hands in the air and quit the relationship straightaway, she decided to program Sadij to denigrate his father, Taib, to weaken the relationship between the two. She thought that this parental alienation game that she did engage in would sap Taib's energy, strength and self-esteem and make him come back; she thought Taib could have stayed just for the child.

However, Taib was adamant that going back to Makiera was just like taking his own life. Makiera then persevered so unremorsefully in her ruthless campaign of vilification and denigration of Taib that she eventually managed to make Sadij's emotional rejection of his father become a reality.

Chapter 10

No one could deny the fact that Sadij was devastated by divorce; he was very young and couldn't understand what was happening, and the social fallout of that unbearable separation on the little kid was significant. The poor boy displayed a lot of impulsive and uncontrollable outbursts and unsettled behaviour when it came to his manner of conduct with others. The dissolution of his parent's marriage had skewed the way he looked at personal relationships and what he thought love was. The divorce of Sadij's parents instilled in him the fear of being forsaken, and that was why he had trouble making friends and getting along with others at some point during his school years.

Sadij's best friend since the nursery school Anatole France 2 at Bois l'Abbé in Champigny-sur-Marne had recently quit talking to him. They never quarrelled and Sadij had never thought that anything had gone wrong. Just before deciding to not speak to Sadij any more, Safih and his girlfriend Chirira had started treating Sadij so horribly. During the breaks in the high school's playground, they just would keep Sadij at arm's length, and the poor young lad had no friends to hang out with. One day, Sadij was determined to pull the plug on their ludicrous conspiracy to unravel their real intentions; while he was walking with long steps hastily and vigorously, he ran smack into Chirira and kindly asked her to set the record straight once and for all.

'I just would like to know why you're turning your back on me. I'm not a weakling and I know I deserve to be treated with respect. All right, spill the beans! Tell it like it is and let's put the whole matter to rest.'

The girl's face turned red from embarrassment as she tried hard to put herself together; she eventually managed to express her opinion frankly, 'You know that's too hard to say, but a rumour is being passed around, the gist of which is your father walked out on you because of your mum's adultery, and our parents ordered us to hold aloof from you.'

'Do you think this is a very pertinent and mature way to end a friendship? Besides, why do I always have to pay for the mistakes made by others?' almost moved to tears, answered the little boy.

'I do apologise for the harm I've caused. Believe me, I didn't mean to hurt you,' ruefully said Chirira.

'Never mind! That's okay!'

From that day on, a feeling of chronic insecurity seemed to have taken hold of Sadij's whole being, for he had become unable to make friends in a relaxed and authentic way. But the truth was that feeling of vulnerability was long taking shape early in the boy's life after having been hurt by his father's departure, and it became more poignant every time he compared himself to his fellow schoolmates and harshly judged himself with regular corrosive interior monologues.

Am I not good enough to make friends? What's wrong with me? Am I not a truly lovable guy? Should I be terrified of having no friends for the rest of my life?

An avalanche of nagging questions, irrational thoughts and fears all came in battalion assailing his brain. The biggest challenge that faced Sadij was how to get rid of his insecurities and build his self-esteem.

Chapter 11

Every time Sadij tried to keep at bay those lice of his emotional stability, Makiera was there to sabotage all efforts at building self-esteem.

On that bright Sunday morning, Sadij was sitting on a small chair getting changed into his gym clothes when suddenly, a coarse voice came clanging from behind, *'The older you get the stronger your physical resemblance to your father becomes, and I'm not pleased with that.'*

'I am what I am and stop comparing me to my dad. You disagree with almost everything I do, from my clothes to my haircut; you always have a problem with everything I do. Now that I'm trying to turn the page and start something new to build my self-esteem, you're just making things more complicated.'

'Come on, boy. Just kidding,' she said, and attempted to atone for that negging she was accustomed to by adding, *'It's just a slip of tongue. You're just making something out of nothing.'*

'I bet you're not joking because this just keeps happening very often and it gets on my nerves. I just don't want to argue. I'm not in the mood for that. I must go now.' The discussion ended with Sadij being upset and storming out of the house.

While jogging, a continuous and uninterrupted flow of thoughts kept crossing his mind.

All those beautiful relationships I read about in novels between mothers and their children were all fiction. My mother hates me and doesn't want to see me around any longer. Maybe she treats me like that because I look like the man she hates most – my father. But her criticisms only make things worse. I just can't stop doing things that keep reminding her of my dad. Every move I make, every step I take, every word I say just makes her go crazy and all she can do is to start calling me names. She keeps insulting me under the guise of constructive criticism; her criticisms are always intended to hurt, not help. Now that I'm trying to keep myself busy doing some sports to forget about my inability to make friends, she just compares me to the man she dislikes most; she's always got something to top my new plans; she all the time tries to one-up me. How can she knock the wind out of her son's sails?

Sadij was so engrossed in his thoughts that he lost track of time. A few minutes later, he retraced his steps, went into the kitchen in his jogging shorts, opened the refrigerator, took a bottle of cold water, gulped it down and headed for the shower. When he was all by himself in his room listening to some music, he received a text message, and it was from Chirira. Sadij felt lonely and there was nothing for him to long for. He had no friends, and the only creature that ought to be by his side was his mother. However, the latter was always picking on him – her main concern was to give her son backhanded compliments. As soon as he read the message *"I need to see you. Catch you at the coffee shop that is close to Carrefour Contact. I'll be waiting."* his face changed colour; he suddenly found himself in an unpleasant and troublesome situation from which extrication was difficult.

Should I go? Or should I stay? he was wondering.

What she had told him the other day about her parents ordering her to keep away from him on account of his mother's dalliances repelled the notion of meeting the girl. He was about to rebuff Chirira's invitation when all of a sudden, a feeling of euphoria coming from nowhere got hold of him – a feeling that was so powerful and so overwhelming.

To be happy, I need intimate bonds, I need to take someone into my confidence, I need to feel like I belong, I need to be able to get and give support, I have to put an end to loneliness.

Then, a peculiar sensation overtook him, pushing him into a situation where he began to doubt whether Chirira was genuinely well-intentioned, kind and helpful.

'Is she worthy of my trust?

He was wavering between two courses of action. At last, the balance was tipped in favour of the heart, and Sadij accepted the invitation. He gave himself some time to get ready; he got dressed, brushed his hair and gave himself a little pep talk in the mirror.

Chapter 12

It was daunting to encounter Chirira who was physically attractive, super smart, high-powered and very popular among her peers. He remembered the first time he ran into her; he was riding his bike, and as soon as he came around a bend, he found a very young girl lying on the ground because her bicycle skidded on a patch of ice, had her leg hurt so badly she couldn't walk. So, Sadij offered to help her get on her feet. That had happened a long time ago before she became his classmate.

But now things were a bit different in that she sent him a text message asking to see him. On his way to meet her, he began chewing the cud, *What would she like to talk to me about? What if she rubs salt into my wounds by telling me again nasty stuff about my mother? Then I would have to see her at school again and again.*

Sadij was devastatingly insecure because Chirira was smarter than him and also because he was a very shy young lad. Since he had a proclivity to avoid human contact with others, he had become an introvert, which had proved to be his undoing when it came to interacting with people. He was so engrossed in his thoughts that he didn't realise he happened to be on the doorstep of the coffee shop, and there was sitting in a corner sipping her lemonade Chirira.

The first date with a girl was a little scary and intimidating for Sadij who was used to being alone most of the time, and now and then he got emotionally drained after spending a great deal of time with others. But he didn't want to be alone any more, and the snag with him was that he had problems interacting with others. This time, he was dead set against being on his own all the time.

Being at close quarters with Chirira did send cold fingers of dread creeping up his spine. Chirira, on the other hand, was an outgoing, expressive and so to speak life-of-the-party girl. She had sharp and defined facial features; her ocean blue eyes sparkled like the stars in a twilight dark sky, her high brows created a beautiful frame for her face. Her slightly upturned nose made her appear more feminine. Her lips looked real. The perfect symmetry along the cupid bow couldn't go unnoticed. When she parted her lips lightly to speak, he just kept waiting in anticipation to see her lips move.

'Hi, how's tricks? Long time, no see. Where have you been hiding?

'Oh, fine, thanks. Oh, you know, keeping busy. That's what happens when you have a baby brother to look after when your mum is away from home. How about you? How are you doing?'

'Oh, you know, just plugging along. Nothing too wild going on around here.'

Sadij just kept staring at her as the petals of her lips parted, almost reluctantly sticking together.

Seeing that Sadij was taciturn, Chirira continued the conversation. *'You're not much of a talker, are you?'*

Sadij forced a smile and said, *'I'm really like this. Does that bother you?'*

'Oh, not at all. I like you the way you are. Besides, you can't change the basic nature of a person. I just want you to

come out of your shell.'

Sadij's eyes lighted up as he tried to account for his being an introverted person.

'You know I'm used to being on my own. I often struggle with socialising normally, it's not always easy for me to come up with witty small talk or introduce myself to new people.' He then stopped talking and spent time figuring out what to say when suddenly Chirira, to make Sadij communicate with her in a relaxing manner, switched gears.

'Can I get you something to drink?'

'Thank you. I'd like an orange juice,' Sadij replied, feeling flattered by Chirira's attention, for he had never felt so special, so loved in his whole life. For the first time in his life, Sadij felt there was someone who would stand by him, no matter the situation. It was precious to have someone that wouldn't make your heart scream.

'You know, Sadij. I'm struggling in my math classes and need to pass and would be grateful to you if you don't mind helping me improve my math grades. Besides, you're mathematically talented. I was enthralled by the different approach you applied to that equation last time when the math teacher asked you to go to the blackboard to explain how you solved the equation.'

When Chirira was complimenting Sadij, the latter was on cloud nine and wouldn't wish to come down soon. Chirira's commendation of Sadij's intellectual talents was a huge unit of love that was being transmitted; it was an incredibly sweet bonding, a social glue that the young lad had never experienced before.

Sadij smiled, took in the compliment and said, *'Oh, thank you, dear friend. You can always bank on me, whatever happens.'*

'I knew I could count on you, buddy.'

Seeing that Sadij had started to open up emotionally, Chirira engaged in some humour.

'How much would you charge for an hour of math class?'

'You got to be kidding me. Of course, you don't need to pay. Come on, what are friends for?'

'You're a true friend. When I called you up, I thought you wouldn't show up, especially after all I had told you. I do apologise. I didn't mean to hurt you.'

'It's okay! Now, I know that you're a lovingly honest person. You don't pull your punches. I mean you just say exactly what's on your mind.'

'I appreciate this because most of the time my being outspoken often gains some enemies along the way. But unlike other guys, at least I stand by what I believe in and am not afraid to speak my mind.'

At this very moment, all the things he usually hated seemed to be fine as long as he was with his love-giving angel. He felt like nothing bad could happen. The joyous feelings that Sadij was experiencing at this moment did have the capacity to overshadow all feelings of sorrow and anguish which he had hitherto undergone. Sadij was desperately in need of feeding on that blissful moment he was going through. How he wished he could stop that very moment! How he wished he could make it last forever. He was distracted from this very sweet reverie by Chirira's voice.

'I must be off, it's getting late. It was nice talking to you. See you later, bye!'

'Take care,' replied Sadij, who was in a daydreaming mood.

Chapter 13

When Sadij returned home, he locked himself in his bedroom, thinking tenderly about every second he had spent with his first love; he impatiently wanted time to go by very swiftly so that he could see her again. She meant a lot to him now and he couldn't do without her. He was utterly submerged by her love. In a word, he didn't want to lose her. She was the only person that understood him. Now, he had a good reason to live. While lying in his bed, he began to picture the way she talked to him and smiled. He could remember seeing a sparkle in those beautiful eyes of hers. But that wasn't fool proof, for some girls could be just friends. Then, a whole batch of nagging questions popped into his mind; *Is she interested in me? Does she feel what I do feel? Does she treat everyone the same way? Does she probably think of me differently?*

Falling in love with Chirira reduced Sadij's stress, relieved his pain and made him happier than ever before. From the first meeting, Sadij started looking at Chirira lovingly. Whenever they got together, he felt his heart flutter, his palms sweat and his mood instantly got better. Indeed, no sign showed she liked him. The young boy was simmering with pent-up romantic emotions. No matter what he was doing to occupy his time, everything seemed to remind him of her. Wherever he went, he just kept thinking of her; what he was feeling was something that couldn't be helped. She just kept popping into his head all the time.

The following day, Sadij didn't have class, and at this same time last week, he had been learning English and doing some math homework. But today, he spent time glancing at his phone to make sure that there was no problem with the telephone line. A few minutes later, he took his phone out again and ascertained that its volume was turned on and not on silent. He then got out of his room to fetch a can of Coke from the kitchen. When he returned to his room, he picked up his phone to ensure he hadn't missed any of her calls or texts. While fumbling with his phone, the sound of the mobile abruptly went off, making him nervous and sending a tingle down his spine. Contrary to his expectations, it was his mother Makiera calling.

'Hi, sweetie! Will do me a favour?'

'I'd be glad to help out,' answered Sadij.

'Will you take the steak out of the freezer, 'cause I'll be home a bit late.'

'No problem!' replied Sadij.

Makiera possessed the knack for influencing and controlling others to her advantage. She could feign niceness to get what she wanted. More often than not, her requests ranged from small, reasonable ones to completely ludicrous. It was as if she was trying to find out how far she could push her son. If ever Sadij rebuffed her requests, she would unleash the hell hounds of blame and culpability on him to coerce him into compliance. But at this point, Chirira was the only ethereal creature that mattered to Sadij. Nevertheless, she hadn't given a ring yet.

He started feeling pangs of self-doubt. *Maybe this lack of self-assurance and faith in myself may cause a lot of problems*

in my relationship with Chirira. I'm afraid of losing her; I'm
afraid of being rejected. I have been dumped by my father, and
I can't take this any more. Do I deserve to be in a relationship
with her? Perhaps, she is too good for me. Sooner or later, she
will realise it and then leave me.

After casting doubt on his self-esteem, Sadij undertook to replay the conversation he had with Chirira yesterday, looking for any hidden meaning in every sentence she uttered, any telltale tokens in her gestures, her smiles and looks.

I remember she keeps sneaking looks at me. That's true.
She wants to look at me but doesn't want me to know it. I catch
her looking at me. I remember she sometime looks away when
caught. So, she's attracted to me; she's interested in me. Why
am I making such a fuss about nothing? She has asked me
questions about my personal life because she finds it
interesting and would like to be part of it. But that doesn't
prove anything because if she likes me, she would at least make
an effort to call me. Or, maybe she's expecting me to give her
a ring.

He swiftly pulled the phone out of his pocket again and, with shaking hands, gave her a buzz. But she didn't pick up his call, and he started getting worried sick again. He cast a glance at his wrist-watch to see whether it was getting late to call her again. It was seven p.m. sharp. He called and called again and again and received no answer. Eventually, he left her a message, *"Really sorry to bother you. I just want to make sure you're okay."*

Chapter 14

Sadij got up early in the morning; he didn't sleep well that night, for he kept tossing and turning in bed. He couldn't get her out of his mind. He trudged to the kitchen, took a thin slice of sandwich bread from the freezer and thawed it in the microwave. Then, he made himself some coffee with sugared concentrated milk, took a chocolate bar from the kitchen shelf, and hurried off to school, hoping he could cross her path. But Sadij had still a few surprises in store. When he got there, he saw her with some guy he had never met before. She was holding hands with him. He wanted to walk over to say hello, but was completely numb; he didn't know what to say; he didn't know what to think; he didn't know if he should greet her or just act like he didn't see her. When she caught sight of him, she coldly introduced him to the guy as a classmate.

Sadij's heart was pounding against his chest too hard and too fast. The wind was knocked out of him. He couldn't spend another second talking to her because he knew he was going to collapse. All that wasn't only about what he saw, but it was about the emotions he was feeling; it was about what Chirira meant to him. It was the place that she had recently had in his heart. Now, he painfully realised that his loved one was with someone else, and the life he thought he would have was no longer possible. A very important part of him passed away; he became a different person than he was a few minutes ago.

He had the premonition that this was coming yesterday because she didn't answer his calls and messages. It was excruciatingly painful how things never turned out the way Sadij thought they would; the unexpected did occur and the poor young man could not live his life as if nothing of it mattered. Only yesterday, Sadij was looking forward to seeing Chirira, because she was his and nobody else's. No one except Sadij knew how painful he felt when the girl he cherished in his innermost heart loved someone else. Sadij was expecting more than what he was likely to get. Wasn't he really overshooting his expectations? Perhaps, he was pushing the relationship forward too fast and made her crowded instead of letting her come to him.

Sadij found it hard to concentrate during class and now and then he gave furtive looks at her sitting on the opposite side of the classroom. She seemed to be unaware of the harrowing suffering she made him endure. When the school bell rang, he took off like a bat out of hell. On his way home, he began mulling over his misery.

The more I hope that there will be a chance that things will go the way I hope they will, the more likely I am to be caught off my guard when that doesn't take place. Why me? What have I done to God to deserve such a fate? Why can't only one of my dreams and hopes come true? She was the one I thought I would end up with. I thought she was the one that would change my entire life; I thought she was the key that would unlock the door to my true happiness. But seeing her holding hands with that guy this morning did break me. I felt lost and lonely.

Chapter 15

Sadij's innocent crush on Chirira, unfortunately, developed into a real obsession that continually forced its way into his consciousness, thus impinging upon his physical and mental well-being. The kind of love that Sadij was experiencing was a one-sided and unrequited one because Chirira was not aware of Sadij's deep and strong romantic affection. The kind of romantic attraction that he felt towards her was mingled with an obsessive need to have that same fascination reciprocated. As soon as Sadij realised the feelings of love he was harbouring for her were not returned, he immersed himself into despondency and loneliness. That wasn't the first time that Sadij had ever been disappointed. His disenchantment went back to the time when he thought that his mother, who was supposed to be the fountain of love, support and care, turned out to be the source of anguish and grief. He locked himself in his room and didn't want to socialise.

At that very moment, Sadij was desperately in need of taking someone into his confidence, in need of snuggling in someone's arms and dumping his purse on him. How he wished his mother could just whisk by and ask how he was doing! But the instant she returned home from work, she dashed into her room to take a shower. She just didn't care a hang about him. One of the happiest moments in her life was when she was by her husband's side; before getting remarried, she hadn't wanted Sadij to be successful and independent because she had always wanted to maintain her sway over him; she would even go to any length just to keep him dependent and under her thumb. From a selfless caretaker of a recently broken family and a seemingly loving mother, Makiera veered to her real self – that of an egocentric person whose main concern was to put her base needs first – thus disregarding the emotional needs of her child. As Mrs Moukafiha, Makiera's mother, used to say to her daughter, *'I guess what's bred in the bone will come out in the flesh.'*

Poor Sadij was sad and eating his heart out, with no one to turn to, to allay his grief; and as the saying goes, "It never rains, but it pours," for Makiera kept – at a time when Sadij was badly in need of consolation – driving a nail in his coffin through her playing favourites with her children. She used to put her golden child Ashraf on a pedestal while smothering the scapegoat Sadij with corrosive criticisms.

The following day, Sadij was sitting in the living room watching a soccer match in which his favourite team Marseilles was playing against Bordeaux when suddenly Ablah, Makiera, and their little child Ashraf came in. As the latter was a musical theatre buff, his mother kept lauding the child's talents.

'O, my dearest son, you were so amazing on the platform. Did you see, Ablah, how the words he spoke were in keeping with his movements?'

'Yeah, sure. I'll never forget the standing ovation he received in the end. I hope you did shoot that unforgettable event with your camcorder,' Ablah said.

'I would be crazy if I hadn't,' replied Makiera.

But how about Sadij, who was very good at soccer? She

had never taken the trouble to watch him play, let alone praise him.

Sadij was a victim of parental favouritism. He could find excuses for his stepfather because Ablah favoured his biological child over his step-child. However, he couldn't stand seeing his mother spending more time with Ashraf, giving him more affection, more privileges and less dressing down. Sadij was a very affectionate and pleasant boy, and his mother was supposed to behave more affectionately towards him. Besides, he had never acted out or engaged in deviant behaviour.

Makiera's display of partiality towards her favoured child Ashraf did have some negative repercussions on Sadij, who had to go through negative outcomes in that he became more depressed, more aggressive and less self-assured. Worse than that, Makiera and her husband had managed to poison the relationship between the children, for they both came to resent and hate one another.

That terrible night, Sadij lay down on the cushioned bed staring at the ceiling and brooding. *I love my mother and I've spent my life searching for her affection and approval, but I have never received any of them. Instead, she keeps scolding me for trivial stuff. In school, I've always had good grades, I have always toed the line and have done what I've been told. Feeling rejected by her hurts a lot; she has always made me feel less loved.*

Makiera and her husband were a lot more blatant about showing more likeness towards Ashraf than Sadij, without being cognisant of the detrimental implications that parental favouritism might have on Sadij. Being the black sheep of the family had made Sadij a very strong and better person.

Part II

Chapter 1

Seeing that his stepdad had never made an effort to get to know or treat him like his own, Sadij had decided to move out of the house before he came of age. Ablah had made it clear from the get-go that he didn't want to see him around and that he wasn't desired. His mother, as usual, had her head stuck up her arse to realise that. One thing Sadij was sure of was that Makiera had always taken her husband's side because he had always taken advantage of the fact that Makiera had no interest in Sadij since the latter kept reminding her of her ex-husband. As a result, Sadij moved into his grandparents' flat and felt as though he was given a new lease of life. At least, Mrs Moukafiha was a lovely, nice woman, who had always been there for Sadij. Her compassionate heart had never failed to emotionally support him when he was desperately in need of his mother's affection.

Nothing could speak to the emotional pain felt by Sadij on two different occasions; as a result of the emotional distress he felt upon discovering Chirira dating another one, and the shock he felt following him being ousted from home by his mother, Sadij was utterly devastated. Oddly enough, he came out of all that all right. No doubt, it was a tough situation, for if a weaker guy were caught in the same situation, they would engage in risky behaviour such as substance use, would not perform well academically or would even end up in trouble with the law throughout their young adulthood.

However, Sadij was an exception. He decided to set goals, and now he had dreams to fulfil. He was determined to toil strenuously, no matter what roadblocks he might run into. The way he viewed hurdles to achieving his goals was amazing because he began considering obstacles as an opportunity to grow and thrive. He, therefore, decided not to let himself be overwhelmed with painful thoughts and excruciating emotions. He realised that love just wasn't enough in that he tried with all his might to make things work with persons that weren't right for him. He found out that striving to make things go right was just energy-depleting.

It was time for him to close a painful chapter in his life and move forward. He was resolved to make the most of his schedule. Before meeting Chirira for the first time, he had carefully managed his study time every week. However, the instant he met Chirira, he failed to adhere to that realistic plan. Now, he decided to prepare his weekly schedule at the beginning of each new week. He wrote down his calendar for each class he had for each week. So, he couldn't wait to take up English lessons again, after a long interruption.

He allotted one hour a day to learn English. He didn't want to juggle multiple and different tasks for fear of ending up being less productive. Studying very hard was not a very efficient diversion from emotional instability, for those unpleasant memories kept bugging Sadij whenever he tried to keep his nose to the grindstone. Some of the painful, emotional memories that Sadij would most like to forget turned out to be the toughest to leave behind, especially the negative comments that he had gotten from his mother.

Whenever he tried to intentionally block off the retrieval of some of those disheartening comments of his mother by focusing and getting engrossed in his studies, they just kept creeping in. But Sadij's motivation to intentionally forget those humiliation-laden insults of his mother and some of his classmates was powerful enough that he more or less managed to cope with the effect of those painful and traumatic experiences that he had been through.

Chapter 2

Graduating from high school with a baccalaureate degree was a feat for a young man born into a family of Moroccan immigrants. His mother originated from Berkane and his father came from Marrakech. Taib came to Paris where he pursued his postgraduate studies at Sorbonne University and was awarded his PhD in American civilization. Perhaps, the young man was predestined to follow in his father's footsteps. When he first started school, he couldn't stop himself thinking how much labour and time he had ahead of him before he could achieve the hoped-for goal. But when he got his baccalaureate, he was astonished by the swiftness with which time had flown; going to the university was a huge accomplishment for a young man coming from one of the disadvantaged neighbours in the Parisian suburbs. Sadij was proud of himself. Candidly speaking, that wasn't a piece of cake, for along the way life was tougher than he had expected. He had experienced moments of self-doubt; there were ups and downs, but he did it.

He knew that this was just the beginning of the real battle that he had to win as far as that whole post-secondary education that was ahead of him was concerned. Though entering the university was extremely exciting, it was also time for Sadij to think about which discipline to choose. After deep reflection on the job opportunities that each program could offer, Sadij chose to major in economics at Paris Diderot University. Attending university was not only about attending classes and studying modules. Sadij realised that learning at the university level had nothing to do with knowledge acquired in high school, for he was picking up worthwhile skills and behavioural competencies such as teamwork, confidence, decision-making, taking initiatives and addressing problems. All those skills that were something new to Sadij would, he believed, prepare him for his future and propel his career.

For the first time in his life, Sadij had stopped being an anonymous sheep in the flock. Gone were the days when he used to be gagged by his high school instructor whenever he dared to ask embarrassing questions. He could remember quite well how his high school teacher had turned him up to ridicule when he suggested a different approach to an equation. At the university, Sadij could dare to be himself; he could be creative and different. In that new environment, his actions did have a purpose and his life had a meaning. He even managed to come out of his shell and made friends.

The only unbearable and unforgettable experience that was etched on his memory was the French tradition in universities known as 'le bizutage'. To become part of a popular group on campus, Sadij was asked to urinate in the amphitheatre before the lecture began, which he vehemently refused. However, this rebuff did stick in the craw of that insane group of students, for they were more determined than ever to get revenge upon him.

On the D-day, some students from the students office threw a party under the guise of welcoming freshmen to campus. So, they contrived a scheme in secret and sent an invitation to Sadij, cordially inviting him to the Freshman

Welcoming Ceremony.

As they knew from the outset that he was a teetotaller, they offered him straight orange juice in which they secretly slipped an illegal drug to take advantage of him. That substance had immediately left Sadij unable to protect himself; he became physically weak and passed out. They administered to Sadij an overdose of cat Valium that made him feel completely detached from his environment and himself. They undressed him and forced him to go away naked to poke fun at him.

The poor naked young man was staggering and unable to maintain normal balance; all of a sudden, he stumbled, fell onto the sidewalk, hit his head and swooned. Fortunately, there was a police patrol moving about that same area for security purposes. When they caught sight of the body lying on the ground, they pulled up the car at the curb and called an ambulance that took him to the hospital. When he came round, he uttered words indistinctly and couldn't remember what happened.

He looked around the room and saw a young woman in white scrubs trying to reassure him that everything was right.

'Where on earth am I? What's going on?'

He attempted to get up, but his leg was being held up by a pulley, and he was wearing a neck brace to prevent extreme forward, rearward and sideways head movement.

'Just relax, young man, we're just putting this device around your neck as a precautionary measure until possible injuries to your neck can be evaluated.'

Sadij was unaware of the extent of the damage done to his neck, and just kept staring at the nurse, who told him that the doctor was coming very shortly. There came along the hospital corridor a tubby middle-aged man with a rubicund countenance. When he got closer to Sadij's cot, he whispered something into the nurse's ear.

The nurse said, *'Oh, not yet!'*

'Well, man, we just don't know who you are. The paramedics said they found you lying unconscious and naked in Boulevard St Michel. Now, if you could just tell us what your name is so that we can fill out the hospital registration form. Could you remember what happened?'

As he was heavily medicated, it caused a slight slur in his voice. *'The last thing I remember is that I was invited to Freshmen Welcoming Ceremony organised by the students office of my university, and I... that's all.'*

The doctor adjusted his spectacles, straightened his white coat and cast dubious glances at Sadij. He finally said, *'The blood test result reveals that there's a high drug level in your blood. Do you remember having drunk something before losing consciousness?'* The doctor wanted to know.

Sadij coughed with a jerk as he was trying to recollect what occurred that night.

'Yeah, I remember a friend offered me an orange juice.'

'I see,' said the doctor. Turning to the nurse in quest of confirmation, he continued, *'You remember some serious hazing cases were admitted to the hospital last year?'*

The nurse nodded her assent. The doctor gave Sadij a withering stare, before continuing his diatribe, *'Every year, college students are injured or even killed due to the folly and lack of a sense of responsibility of few students; I just can't understand how come they regard making their peers go through some humiliating rituals such as drinking and violence as fun and games.'*

While the medical practitioner was speaking, Sadij was listening spellbound. Then he started asking Sadij a series of questions regarding his medical history.

'*Do you have any allergies?*'

'*No!*' answered Sadij.

'*Have you undergone any past surgeries?*'

'*Never, sir,*' Sadij said.

'*Do you smoke or drink alcohol?*'

'*No, I don't,*' replied Sadij; he seemed to be fed up with the interrogation.

While Sadij was lying down, the doctor was feeling his abdomen; then he took a listening device that he hung around his neck to listen to Sadij's lungs and ordered Sadij, '*Take a deep breath, will you?*'

Then, he used that same stethoscope to listen to Sadij's heartbeat to make sure there were no abnormal sounds.

When the doctor had the physical examination done, he asked Sadij, '*Is there any member of your family we can reach by phone?*'

Sadij felt embarrassed and ashamed because he didn't want anyone to know what befell him. '*I hope you don't mind, sir, but would it be possible not to let my family know?*'

Upon hearing this, the doctor could no longer hide his surprise. '*Why? Besides, the paramedics brought you naked to the hospital. So, we need to contact a family member so that they can bring you some clothes to put on. See?*'

Eventually, he gave them his grandmother's cell phone number.

When Mrs Moukafiha received the bad news, she at first tried to give herself time to digest and process the unexpected information. She couldn't believe what she had heard on the phone. She took a few deep breaths and attempted to calm herself. *'It won't wash, it won't wash to say that something terrible happened to Sadij.'*

All kinds of disastrous scenarios assailed her, and she jumped to the absolute worst upshots in her mind. She just didn't know what to do. *'Do I need to keep Makiera informed about it? What good would it be? She has never cared a hang about the poor boy.'*

To discard bias and watered-down information that might be more hearsay than factual, she decided to go straight to the hospital. Before doing so, she immediately took some of Sadij's clothes and got on the high-speed train linking Paris to the suburbs. On her way to the hospital, she was condemning herself and wallowing in guilt; it was really difficult for her to get past holding herself accountable for what had happened. She felt she'd got a huge share of responsibility in the bad news because Sadij was in her custody.

She was frustrated because she felt she had failed to bring Sadij up, full of eagerness to go out and take on the world; nevertheless, she knew she had always been present at every juncture in the boy's life; she felt it in her bones that she had given him the absolute conviction that she loved him thoroughly, without reservation, no matter what he might do and no matter what might happen. But now the time had come when he had to take responsibility for his life. When Sadij saw Mrs Moukafiha, he was really upset, embarrassed and didn't know what to say when asked to relate what transpired.

He was mainly ashamed of the humiliating situation he found himself in, for his grandmother had always put him on a pedestal. It was really painful for him to think that he didn't come up to her expectations. Seeing her grandson there having his leg supported and lifted by a leg sling in conjunction with the hoist, she was shocked and scared. When she realised how embarrassing it was for Sadij to talk about what had happened, she ditched the idea altogether. Telling his grandmother the whole truth just gave him the creeps.

A few minutes later, Mrs Moukafiha took the nurse aside and tried to talk to her privately in an attempt to find out what Sadij had been trying to conceal. When she got a succinct account of the whole incident, she felt some relief. She was told that Sadij could not leave the hospital right now and that he needed to stay in it for at least one night. She then returned to the hospital room where Sadij was and told him, *'I'm running to the store nearby. Tell me what you need and I'll bring it to you.'*

'No, thank you, dear Ma,' replied Sadij.

To which she responded while patting his shoulder, *'But you're not going to starve to death because you will be staying here till tomorrow; therefore, you need to have something to eat. By the way, if you need me to pick some stuff up and bring them to the hospital for you while I'm coming back tonight, I can.'*

'I don't think that's necessary 'cause the doctor told me that I'll probably be leaving the hospital tomorrow afternoon.'

'Be right back.'

Chapter 3

The hazing experience that he'd been through not only scarred him, but it left a long-lasting impact on his future relations with his mates, his self-esteem and mental health. Sadij was too alarmed when he heard other cases of hazing that involved deaths. The effects of that nightmarish and worst experience of his life were still visible today, for Sadij suffered from sleeping problems, eating disorders, anxiety and misgiving. He began to call into question the goal of hazing itself; for him, that stupid ceremony of getting initiated into college was not at all meant to, as some college students averred, bring students together and create a bond, but rather a terrible and dangerous thing that struck fear into the hearts of scapegoats like him.

Sadij came to college full of hopes, but his high expectations came tumbling down in the wake of that ridiculous rite of passage that any new student had to go through to fit in and belong. That terrible incident did not only make him sick, but it also took away from him his tenuous sense of trust that he was hoping to restore in the university.

From that day forth, Sadij realised that the easiest thing to do was to say nothing, agree with everybody and keep out of others' hair. He knew that it was downright next to impossible to change people. It eventually dawned upon him that the best approach to adopt was to change the way he perceived and reacted to whomever he would have to deal with in the future.

For that, he created his personal space and mentally drew its boundaries. He realis-ed that if he didn't act that way, then he would be pushed over by others, and might, unfortunately, end up living apart from others like a hermit, and that wasn't what he wanted. The trouble with Sadij was that he was reared to be kind, friendly and put the needs of others before his own. Now, he started to realise that being a people-pleaser was a waste of good intentions, for it entailed using up too much vain energy; he was a very tender-hearted and very sensitive creature that hated speaking honestly and offending people by telling them the truth because he had always found that the truth sucked to hear.

That ugly hazing experience taught him that it was high time he made some shifts in his life concerning his relationship with other people through speaking his mind. One day just as he was about to go home for lunch, Valerie, a student in the same class as Sadij, made bold to accost him, as he was passing through the wide-open gates of the Diderot University, and asked him, *'Mind if I go with you to the dining hall?'*

There was a moment of hesitation before Sadij could muster up the courage; finally, he found his voice and replied while remaining appropriate, diplomatic and respectful of her, *'Thank you so much for the invitation, I appreciate it and it means a great deal, but I've got to boogie 'cause my mother is expecting me for lunch. May be some other time. Okay?'*

Valerie said, *'Of course!'* She bid him goodbye and went away.

Sadij didn't know how she felt about it, but at least he said what he felt, which removed so much anxiety and was likely to promote intimacy and trust between the two. For the first time in his life, Sadij had managed to say no clearly and without making a big deal about it.

Chapter 4

Gone were the days at high school when Sadij would take everything on the fly, he had now to cope with the demanding workload of the university that required some serious planning. So, he was more determined than ever before to apply himself to the assignments given by his instructors, especially when one of his teachers took a fellow student to task for having botched up his homework. *'A serious work cannot be done in one night, Laurent. Besides, it's been two weeks now since I've given you the assignment.'*

Sadij realised that procrastinating and putting off doing his work would bring about a great source of stress, which was not what he wished for. His main aim was to achieve high results. That was why he handed in all his assignments on time and didn't have to struggle to finish them up at the last minute. Managing his schedule did make his life easier and earned him the respect of all his teachers. Sadij would at times feel guilty whenever he happened to waste some time aimlessly. For him, time was money. He used to say to himself that, *'A student that doesn't care is bound to fail, come what may.'*

Having said that, Sadij was not a workaholic that had a compulsive and unrelenting addiction to work; on the contrary, he managed to earmark some time for listening to music and going out for a walk. He knew that there would always be work to do even when school was done. Therefore, he needed to take some rest from time to time.

Of all his fellow students, François was the slyest, because whenever he was asked whether he did the assignment, he would deceive his classmates through his famous phrase *'I haven't started yet!'* Lying was part of François' life. Later on, François explained to Sadij that lying kept him safe and protected him from the evil eye. His unshakable belief in the curse of the evil eye stemmed from the conviction that achieving great success and recognition would simply attract the envy of his fellow students and that would undo his good fortune. Sadij and Valerie were shocked and appalled to learn that a somewhat smart student could still believe in such superstitious myths.

Valerie commented on this while chatting with Sadij, *'There's no scientific evidence behind this myth. It's more of a belief in backward traditions than a scientific truth; I guess there's absolutely no ground proof for this trash. Do you see where I'm coming from?'* She was looking straight into Sadij's eyes, attempting to secure his approval.

'I see what you mean. Of course, believing in such regressive ideas is a lot of baloney. First, science disproves this, for the mere reason that an eye emits no light, no laser beams and no evil intent. On the contrary, the eye is a passive receptor of light. Guess what? If one tries to cast an evil eye on the sun, one will end up getting burned,' said Sadij, who was chuckling with laughter.

'Wow! It doesn't get any better than this. You hit the jackpot, Sadij,' said Valerie, expressing her approval.

'Look here, Valerie. That guy has got it all wrong. No pun intended this time. After they made him, they broke the mould.'

The use of positive humour by Sadij did cheer up Valerie, who couldn't help laughing. His being funny made him more desirable as a potential mate.

Chapter 5

Sadij began to see some flickers of hope hovering over the horizon, telling him that this time his relationship with Valerie had greater chances of withstanding the long haul. But he didn't know for sure what the future might hold in store for him. For the first time in his life, there was someone who could have his back, and that was Valerie. They both got along with each other, studied together and did a bunch of stuff together. She managed to offer him the peace of mind he had been looking for by increasing his happiness, reducing his stress and diminishing the mental suffering he'd long been suffering from.

Before meeting Valerie, Sadij used to have some preconceptions about French people; he used to think that they were all of them racist and xenophobic. He was dead wrong, for Valerie had a few friends and neighbours of colour with whom she regularly socialised, and in the discussions she had had with Sadij, she talked very often about the evils of discrimination and prejudice.

One day, when she was having lunch with Sadij, the latter broached the topic and related to her a very traumatic experience he had been through.

'I remember it just like it was yesterday. I was walking down the street, and when I approached a French woman, she unconsciously pulled her child nearer to her. I'll tell you another one, but don't get all bent out of shape. As soon as I hopped into the subway, again a European woman

immediately and perhaps unconsciously cast a hostile stare at me and shifted her bag from one hand to the other. She perhaps thought I was a pickpocket.'

Valerie remained silent for a while and then reacted, *'I understand what you're saying. It gets on my nerves to see that Arabs and Muslims suffer from discrimination, stigmatisation and exclusion from employment and other areas of life. I believe that the dehumanisation of Arabs in France is due to some negative stereotyping; the most disgusting thing about it is that the extreme right party unceasingly portrays Muslims as a threat to the European way of life. But you know, Sadij, they constitute just a minority. Most French are not racist. Xenophobes are only people who haven't travelled abroad to discover other cultures, and therefore they remain narrow-minded.'*

Seeing that she was trying to empathise with him, he said with a voice loaded with emotion, *'Well, it's true that racism, xenophobia and intolerance are pretty much common in all societies, but Valerie... you can't imagine what it feels like to be a permanent victim of racial prejudice and intolerant attitudes. It hurts, and I sometimes get the impression that this isn't the place where I have to be. I feel I don't belong here... and I... I...'*

He was about to finish articulating his innermost thoughts when Valerie butted him in, *'Come on! Sadij, don't let this get you down! You can lay that notion to rest because I'll always be there for you. What are friends for?'* She took hold of his hand as she uttered these soothing words. After that, she cast a glance at her wristwatch and said, *'We need to get going if we don't wish to miss out on Prof. Gautier's lecture.'*

'Yeah, you're right!' They both got up, put their trays next to the cutlery drawers of the dishwasher and hurried off to the university.

Chapter 6

Sadij realised that embracing new cultures within the confines of the Diderot University would undoubtedly make him grow and become an open-minded bloke. Rubbing shoulders with students coming from other countries would most likely expand his horizon and help him learn other skills. On weekends, one of the forty international student residences that pertained to the International University City of Paris that was located in the fourteenth district of Paris would throw a party, thus allowing foreign students to get to know one another. It was Jaaba, a Moroccan student taking up residence in the House of Morocco, who put the bug in Sadij's ear about making new friends hailing from different parts of the globe.

That Saturday, it was the Danish Foundation's turn to host a party to allow the students who were stressed out to have some fun. Having a good time at the end of a very laborious week would probably give the student's brain permission for learning to happen. Sadij knew that being stressed out would probably prevent him from reaching his academic best.

Lately, he and Valerie had been working on a joint project that they had to submit in due time. So, he stayed up late last night administering the last touches to that laborious task. He was pulling his hair out trying to revamp the work to come up to the expectations of his instructor. To relieve their tensions from studying, they headed out to the Fondation Danoise.

They walked across the lobby that led to the living room where there was so much noise going on, Sadij hesitated, grasped Valerie's hand and pulled her towards him as if he wanted to prevent her from going in.

She then turned and asked, *'What's up?'*

Sadij looked very uneasy and stayed quiet for a while, then he spilled the beans, *'I can't stand it.'*

'Cut to the chase. I didn't dig what you mean,' she replied, looking perplexed because she couldn't make out why he changed his mind so swiftly.

'This place stinks. It's not my style.'

'What are you talking about? Wait a second. Before coming to this fucking place, you were so excited. Just lay it on the line, for we're not going to stand here all day,' she angrily said, urging him to come up with a cogent reason.

'You know, Valerie, it's really hard to explain. This kind of shitty atmosphere reminds me of that terrible experience I went through in that damned hazing event,' he explained, heaving a deep sigh.

With difficulty, she pulled his hand, trying to make him move forward, and said, *'Listen! your explanation doesn't just make the grade. Besides, you're letting the world pass you by. This time, you're not alone. Come on. Mellow out. I swear to God. Everything is gonna be fine. Just take things as they come.'*

With these reassuring words, Sadij capitulated, for he knew that this time he was in safe hands. As they made their way through the dancing crowd, music drifted through to him, jarring on his nerves; everyone seemed hungry for their fill of disco dancing and passionately danced to amplified pop records, compered by a crazy turntablist that kept pulling faces at the crowd on the dance floor.

Almost all students seemed off the chain and just romped in tune with numbers like 'Night Fever', 'Staying Alive', and 'You Can't Hurry Love'.

As soon as 'Careless Whisper' was played, a young man stepped in the dance floor and asked Valerie, *'Do you know who does this song?'*

Valerie was taken aback by this question. Then after a moment of hesitation, she answered, *'Yeah, it's George Michael.'*

As she was about to dodge through the crowd, the presumptuously forward and impudent man took her hand and said, *'Care to dance?'*

To which she politely replied, *'I'm seeing someone else.'* No sooner had she finished her sentence than Sadij came to her rescue, shouting, *'Are you all right?'*

'I'm sorry, I can't hear what you're saying,' she said in a loud voice, as the noise of the music around her was deafening.

Sadij drew closer to her and whispered in her ear, *'I said are you okay?'*

She eventually said, *'Yeah, I'm just fine.'*

She didn't wish to kick up a hell of a row about that young man's brashness, because she knew that Sadij would be offended.

Afterward, she went off at a tangent and started talking about the place. *'I guess there's not enough room to swing a cat; and I need some elbow room.'*

Valerie looked very pretty in that smashing dress she was wearing and couldn't go unnoticed. A very handsome young student kept waving at Valerie, and Sadij asked Valerie, *'Who's that guy waving at you?'*

'I don't know. I've never seen him before.'

Tired of waving his hand, the young man walked up to her and, to Sadij's dismay, the tipsy guy uttered slurred words, *'Don't I know you from somewhere?'*

'No, I mean, not that I know of,' she replied expeditiously, attempting to get rid of the guy.

But the latter went too far, *'What's a nice girl like you doing in a place like this?'*

Pushed to the limit of her patience, she said, *'This is more than I can take. That blows my mind.'*

Steering Sadij to another part of the living room for fear that he might come to blows with the guy, she said, *'Look, Sadij, you have to learn to roll with the punches; there's nothing we can do to change things. I think we had better go while the going is good.'*

Very disappointed, they left the place and walked side by side through the quiet and pitch-dark alley that led to the closest subway stop. It was getting late, and Sadij didn't want Valerie walking home alone.

When Sadij offered to see her home, she turned and looked at him and with an ethereal smile said, *'Oh, that's kind of you, but I don't want to disturb you, 'cause the subway stops just in front of my flat at Republic Avenue, the main street of the tenth district of Paris, which is where I'm taking up residence now.'*

But Sadij was getting worried that something bad might befall her, he then kept insisting. However, Valerie seemed adamant not to give in. So, he nodded his head and followed her with his eyes as she went down the stairs of the underground station, but something inside of him didn't want her to go home alone. He then walked over to her and beseeched her to let him accompany her home. Valerie was extremely delighted to see that there was someone concerned about her safety.

She then said, *'Look, Sadij, I really appreciate it, but I've been taking the subway for a long time now, and nothing bad ever happened to me.'*

Sadij was afraid that he may have frightened her and decided to let her do what she thought was good for her. He eventually said in a warm and tender voice, *'Okay, but will you do me a favour that will set my mind at rest?'*

She looked at him and asked him curiously, *'What would that favour be?'*

He solicitously replied, *'Call me when you get home?'*

'I'll call you, I promise.'

Chapter 7

As soon as she arrived home, she gave him a buzz to let him know that she had arrived safely, and wished him good night. That reassuring call had set him thinking about the kind of person Valerie was.

She's a straightforward person and isn't like people that beat around the bush. That girl has strong moral principles in that she turned down several guys' advances at that party. She's therefore trustworthy. This is a quality that is getting scarce nowadays. True integrity is getting lost, and all the girls I've met so far are just faking it. She took responsibility for her actions and chose to do the right thing, especially when she avoided telling me what that arrogant guy at the party had told her. Besides, she's not selfish at all because she doesn't put her needs above those of others... this is crystal clear. I asked to see her home, I even insisted, but she refused. Valerie is an angel.

All those positive and pleasant thoughts about Valerie had caused Sadij to become so relaxed that he drifted gently and peacefully to sleep.

Before meeting Valerie, Sadij had been unsure of what to look for in a girl, and what kind of good qualities that he truly deserved to have in any relationship, because he had grown up watching Makiera, his mother, acting out indecent and disgraceful patterns. That mother that should normally serve as a good example for her son to follow or even emulate was offensive to accepted standards of decency and propriety. Valerie stood as a foil to his mother. Valerie was a girl Sadij could have faith in, and without trust, Sadij would have no solid foundation on which to found a solid emotional intimacy that was to last. So, the potential for Sadij to get hurt this time had abated. Now, he knew he had someone he could rely on, someone that could come through for him in time of woe and distress. Their relationship wasn't at all susceptible to tension and dubiety as most personal relationships of his time were. Sadij knew that Valerie, unlike him, opened up to him, and therefore, it would be downright asinine of him to break her trust and disappoint her. Valerie was an authentic girl and Sadij didn't have to worry about how she felt about him because she was the kind of person that said what she felt; and this did away with so much anxiety that Sajid had been suffering from, and accordingly contributed to the flourishing of their relationship that was based on mutual trust.

Chapter 8

After having been dating Valerie for a little over six months, Sadij was head over heels in love with her and decided to introduce her to his mother. However, when he weighed the pros and cons of doing so, he started having second thoughts about the idea itself.

What if she discovers the kind of person my mother is? What if she finds out that my mother is manipulative of anybody that comes into contact with her? What will she think if she ever knows that my mother is married to another man? Will she change her mind about me if she discovers that my parents divorced when I was five years old?

Sadij could still remember the suffering he had endured living with his mother and step-father; he wouldn't forget being wrongly yelled at and harassed by both of them; he could also remember catching his mother oftentimes saying bad things about him to someone else. *How could she judge others and despise them as if she were an immaculate angel?*

In her dealings with her son, Sadij, Makiera's motto was always, *'My way or the highway'*, and the poor Sadij had either to comply with her wanton desires or else be excluded. *What if Valerie sees through my mother's true colours? Will she let me down if she ever finds out that my mother is narcissistic?*

All those obnoxious memories completely repelled the idea of ever introducing the most beloved person in his life to his toxic mother. Sadij didn't want Valerie to get to know his mother's true colours because he didn't want to lose the only person that had put a smile on his face.

After his failed relationship with Chirira, Sadij had, at last, met the girl of his dreams. The two of them did hit it off; when any passer-by caught glimpse of the two walking down the streets of Paris, he would admit that they were naturally friendly, well-suited and made for each other. They studied and revised together, and if an assignment came in, they both would get it done and out of the way; sometimes, they would pull an all-nighter to study for the exam. Getting homework done without the least procrastination made it easier for them to manage the rest of the time they had available. They had spent most of their study time at Valerie's apartment. And they loved spending all their free time together. They would go to the cinema and watch a movie. Sadij seemed to love everything about her; she seemed to possess something Sadij couldn't tell that enabled her to fascinate people and get them to like her. In short, things went off so incredibly well for Sadij that he decided to introduce her this time to his grandmother, Mrs Moukafiha.

As the day set for introducing Valerie to Mrs Moukafiha drew closer, Sadij was very anxious and feared that his grandmother might not like Valerie because she came from a different religious and cultural background. Sadij had always had a good relationship with his grandmother; she had always turned out to be supportive of anything he did. However, he was worried sick about her potentially articulating any red flags that he had previously conjectured. Sadij started the process of vaguely telling his grandmother about his fellow student a week before the long-awaited moment; he didn't mention that she was French. He only said that she was a very serious-minded student that he appreciated.

Mrs Moukafiha made couscous and was ready to welcome her guest. What Sadij had feared the most did happen; Valerie wasn't warmly received by his grandmother.

As soon as Valerie came into the flat, the whole expression of Moukafiha's countenance changed.

Sadij tried to ease the tension that was building by introducing his fellow student to his grandmother, '*Grandma, I'd like you to meet my friend Valerie.*'

While the latter reached out to shake the old lady's hand, Moukafiha kept her arms crossed. Valerie immediately realised that Mrs Moukafiha wasn't a fan of her and that her hopeful new relationship wouldn't go too far.

Meanwhile, Sadij wished he had never brought her to make acquaintance with his bigoted grandmother. Valerie pretended to be enjoying the company of the old witch because she didn't want Sadij to feel how crummy she felt.

'*I've been wanting to meet you for some time. Sadij has told me so much about you. So we finally meet face-to-face. It's a pleasure to have finally met you.*'

The old hag spoke to Valerie while looking elsewhere, '*What was your name again?*'

Valerie answered with a lovely smile on her face, '*My name's Valerie.*'

The old sorcerer cast a hostile glance at Valerie and said, '*Well, listen, Miss Valerie, I've taken the trouble to rear that young man standing right in front of you while his mother is painting the town red.*'

Sadij's face flushed with both embarrassment and shame, and said in a very shaky voice, '*Come on, Grandma, you've screwed it up. You just don't know what you're talking about.'*

The old witch answered back, *'You... you don't know your ass from your elbow.'*

Sadij was about to fly into a rage but pulled himself together and said to his grandma, *'Please, snap out of it,'* and turning to Valerie, he ruefully said, *'I do apologise for the inconvenience that I've caused you. If only I could turn back the hands of time. It's all my fault.'*

This sad situation got Valerie thinking about the strain in which the discussion was getting bogged down; she, therefore, intervened to calm tempers and reduce friction. *'Get a load of this. I just don't want to act like a busybody and pry into the affairs of your family. But I think you both had better pull yourselves together. We're here to have a good time and get to know each other. Right?'*

She said this knowing down deep inside that her efforts to create a new bond wasn't going the way she had previously expected. She took some steps towards Mrs Moukafiha, but the latter wasn't in the least interested in listening, let alone talking to her. The old and bigoted witch purposely distanced herself from Valerie, who couldn't understand why the old woman was so cold towards her. She tried to consider how she could change the way she was handling the situation so as not to invite any further antagonism.

However, when she saw Mrs Moukafiha looking away from her while talking, she realised that the toxic woman didn't like her. She then decided not to drive herself crazy trying to get the manipulative old lady's thumbs-up. At the same instant, Sadij was bewildered by his grandma's lack of respect for Valerie. He then tried to bring her to her senses and said, *'Look here, Grandma. I see what you mean, but Valerie is the kindest and most well-bred person I have ever met in my life. Take my word for it. She's always been supportive of me.'*

Upon hearing this, the old hag tried to annoy her grandson and said, *'Quit pulling my leg, I know there isn't any French or European girl that conforms to the religious standards of behaviour and morality. Besides, we're Muslims and we don't have the same values as Christians.'*

That was the last straw for Sadij, who had no intention of taking the red flags that his grandma was bringing to his attention into consideration. He was determined not to let what she had said get to him because, at the end of the day, he was the one who knew what was good for him. When push came to shove, Sadij knew which party to side with.

'What you've just said doesn't matter to me because I still respect you, but I will never let anyone ruin what I have and love. And thanks for your invitation and for the warm welcome you gave my friend.'

The old sorcerer stood speechless for a long moment, doing nothing but staring at her grandson, who was for the first time sticking for the girl he couldn't do without. Sadij tuned out his grandma and vowed to stand up to her shenanigans. To prevent the situation from getting completely out of control, Valerie endeavoured to straighten things out.

'I'm afraid, Mrs Moukafiha, but I don't think you've got the facts straight. Read my lips. Sadij and I are just friends. Right? Allow me to tell you this… He's like the brother I never had.'

Valerie felt she was up the creek without a paddle, and that giving time and being patient with that old witch was utterly pointless; she took her handbag and said, *'I must call it quits but thanks anyway.'*

She went away leaving Sadij behind. The poor chap followed her and tried to catch up with her, but seeing that she was walking so quickly, he kept calling her, but the young girl, hurt and disappointed, didn't look back. He ran after her, cut her off from the entrance to the metro, and took her aside to speak with her privately.

'I'm just mortified, Valerie. Words can't describe how sorry I am. I just don't know how that could have happened. Is there anything I can do to make it up to you? I throw myself upon your mercy.'

Valerie's anger didn't seem to abate, notwithstanding the apologies made by Sadij. She declined his apologies. *'How would you expect your apology to benefit me? Your grandmother has shown a total lack of respect. I just need to be alone. Please, just give me a break, will you?'*

She went down the stairs that led to the metro, and shoved her way through the hectic crowd.

Chapter 9

Sadij was acutely cognisant of the fact that having a serious-minded and well-mannered girlfriend was something that was getting scarce, especially at a time when flighty and pretty girls in Paris could have as many lovers as they wanted at the same time; dating in the 'City of Lights' was a nightmare, for the erratic fickleness with which most girls in Paris were imbued impelled them to change their affections and attachments very often.

Once a girl came across a good man, she then began to believe that she could find someone even better out there, so she kept changing boyfriends. Sadij knew that most girls there treated relationships like clothing, for they donned several garments until they found the appropriate size. But he didn't want to waste his time thinking about someone who couldn't care less. He was rather a satisfier willing to have a long-lasting relationship, and Valerie was the perfect girlfriend he had been dreaming of. However, all that he had been building from the bottom up did collapse in the wink of an eye. He didn't expect that his grandma could get in the way of him feeling happy.

To keep his relationship with Valerie afloat, he decided to resolve the issue by communicating with her. The next morning, he met her in the refreshment room sipping her morning coffee.

He greeted her, *'How are you this bright morning?'*

'Fair to middling,' she replied and continued drinking coffee gingerly and delicately.

In a soothing voice, he said, *'I understand how you feel. I just want to apologise, and tell you that this will never happen again.'*

Vexed by Sadij's pathetic attempt at reconciliation, she said, *'I'm sorry to disillusion you, but it will be a cold day in hell when I let you take me to one of your relatives next time.'*

Feeling that he was really in trouble and that he might lose Valerie once and for all, Sadij made a last-ditch effort to woo her back, *'For Heaven's sake, just simmer down. I admit that I have created this ugly situation, so I must endure it. My grandma is an old woman that stubbornly resists change and clings to a sort of... how shall I say this... Yeah, she's, in a word, a bigoted person.'*

Valerie requested Sadij to stop that needless talk. *'Will you please cut the crap! I'm not taking things over-personally, but can't you see that when she first saw me, she wasn't in the least interested in being around or talking to me? She seemed to be distracted and disconnected when I was speaking and trying to engage with her. Besides, she didn't seem to have an ounce of respect for me, because normally people talk to each other in ways that don't debase or belittle. Just give me an explanation of what she meant by her saying French girls don't abide by virtuous conduct. This is a shockingly monstrous affront.'*

The more Valerie recollected what had transpired, the angrier she got. Sadij felt helpless and didn't know how to deal with the pressure that was mounting. He was acutely aware of the fact that the pressures he was experiencing came in the first place from his own family and also from differences in culture and unfulfilled expectations. He tried to do his best to keep his relationship with Valerie afloat, but in vain, for the young girl was deeply lacerated.

He attempted to talk with her to figure out the stuff that was important to each of them, and the things that weren't such a big deal, but there seemed to be no chance of making her change her mind. She was inexorably determined to take a bit of a step back. But before bidding Sadij goodbye, she wanted to set something straight. *'Before I go, will you tell me what you said to your grandmother about the kind of the relationship that exists between us?'*

Upon hearing this, Sadij stood motionless, with trembling lips and shaking hands, staring at the ground, then a few seconds later, he managed to gather his wits and began to think about what to say. *'Of course, I said we're just friends.'*

She gave a deep sigh of relief and said, *'Well, that's good to hear.'*

She cast a glance at her watch and exclaimed, *'Oh, it's time to go. The lecture started five minutes ago.'*

They both walked out of the refreshment room and made for the amphitheatre.

Chapter 10

That evening, Sadij trudged home, head bowed, feeling a burning knot starting to swell in his heart; it was as if he had failed a tremendously important exam. He felt disappointed by the only person he cared about; he had been deluding himself all along with false hopes, mistakenly believing that she cared for him as much as he did. But when she told him they were just friends, he felt a relentless dagger stabbed right into his heart. That rejection could have inflicted more damage to Sadij's psychological well-being had Valerie coldly or at best sympathetically rebuffed Sadij's attempt at sharing his adoration with her.

Fortunately for the young man, he kept that euphoric and tremendous unrequited attachment hidden down deep inside. She would have taken him for a jerk had he told her how he felt, though he desperately had had an intense and burning desire to do so. And he might even have fantasised about doing so.

In the wake of that unpleasant encounter with Sadij's grandmother, Valerie had become frequently distant, uninterested and almost unapproachable. Sadij longed for things to be the way they once were between them and found it hard to come to terms with the change in their relationship. However, he kept idealising her and loving her solitarily, even though he had been utterly trounced by the unbearable realisation that his heart was overflowing with intense and warmest feelings that would never be shared, or mutual. The ecstatic and intimate feelings that he went on cherishing in his innermost heart, unfortunately, existed in a vacuity. He couldn't resist those fantasies of reciprocity that kept crossing his mind; though it was make-believe, he was able to undergo a marvellous turn-on at least on the level of his imagination. That unrequited love had completely robbed poor Sadij of his reason and his gumption.

So, he gave himself over to fantasies to fulfil his pious hope. *She may eventually love me back, who knows? What can I do to make her return my love? Maybe she secretly loves me, and she's hiding it out of shyness. Or perhaps, she just needs some time to get to know me better.*

To get a handle on the problem, he decided to drop in on his friend Jaaba to confide in him, because he felt he could no longer eat his heart out on his own.

After relating the whole story to his trusted friend Jaaba, the latter said, *'You're off your rocker. How can you be so stupid?'*

Looking perplexed, Sadij inquired, *'What do you mean? Please cut to the chase.'*

Jaaba, fiddling with his spectacles as they slid down his nose, put his left hand on Sadij's shoulder and said in an earnest tone, *'I'm talking to you like a brother, you know I've been dating nymphs for a while, and I can see through all the tricks they're up to.'*

Sadij getting the drift responded bluntly, *'If you think that Valerie looks like the girls you date, you've got another think coming.'*

Jaaba continued his tirade, *'Let me just finish what I've to say and make myself pretty clear. Okay? Do you want a bit of useful advice?'* Sadij nodded his head in assent. *'First, step back from this girl.'*

Sadij interrupted him, shouting out, *'What? You've gone over the edge.'*

Jaaba could no longer bear his friend's mind being overtaken by intense passion; he proceeded with his speech, *'I guess you're only hearing what you want to hear, and you're pissing me off. You think you're so smart. Get off your high horse.'* Jaaba took a deep breath, and said, *'I know it's none of my business, but I think your goose is cooked.'*

A frown creased Sadij's brow, as he couldn't catch on to what his friend was saying, *'I'm not sure I follow.'*

Jaaba carried on his explanation, *'Well, what I'm saying is as plain as the nose on your face. She just wants to dump you… troll for another guy while keeping you tethered to her fishing line. Don't give her the chance to do it! And, above all, stop deluding yourself with the false hope that she'll change her mind. You'll only be wasting your time. Do not allow her to manipulate your extended false hope! Right? Besides, you said she's avoiding you like the plague. Listen, buddy. It's time for some serious self-care. I mean do have some pride, my friend, and never be a doormat she can trample upon. Okay?'*

Sadij looked helpless and sought Jaaba's advice, *'What am I supposed to do? Please tell me what to do and have done with it.'*

Claiming that what he was saying was crystal clear, Jaaba mockingly inquired, *'Do I need to paint you a picture?'*

Sadij then expressed ignorance, *'Like I would know.'*

The way Jaaba was discussing the issue showed that he was well-versed in personal relationships; he then continued his argument, *'Get a load of this. Try to be happy. Make some new friends. Date other girls. Submerge yourself in some new activities. If you act that way, you will be happier and more successful with girls. But if you go on acting like a pushover, she will take advantage of you. Get my drift?'*

Expressing ignorance, Sadij replied, *'You got me stumped. Over my dead body, I'm not playing that game, Jaaba.'*

The latter expressed indifference. *'Well, it doesn't matter to me. I'm just trying to help, but if you wish to fall into her trap and get hurt, this is your problem.'*

He stopped talking and stared closely at Sadij, who was really in a quandary as to what to do to win Valerie's love back. He then said, *'My dear friend, you look like you've been to hell and back, but the issue is so simple. Let me make myself perfectly clear. Are you still interested in keeping her as a friend no matter how personally excruciating that may be?'*

Sadij replied straightaway, *'Of course! She means so much to me, and I can't imagine myself breaking up with her. That would be a suicidal thing to do.'*

Jaaba got exasperated by Sadij's unreasoning love for Valerie, and shouted, *'Enough is enough. My gut tells me that this malicious girl is just taking you up on your offer to be a friend to kind of fill in the blank; where's your head, buddy? That girl is leading you around by the nose. Come on, what planet are you on?'*

And the way Sadij looked at Jaaba when the latter told him a few home truths! If looks could kill… If looks could kill… What a hostile and angry look!

'Listen up! Be open to new things. If you encounter a new damsel, jump at it.'

Sadij, this time beside himself with ire, exclaimed, *'Cut*

the gub!'

Jaaba asked Sadij to relax, *'Chill out, my friend. You know I'll go to bat for you. If there's anything I can do to help, please let me know. Okay? I'm getting a bit tired now. Let's call it a day. So long!'*

Chapter 11

Sadij felt let down by Valerie, who was the only person on whom he could rely for support as he was all by himself; during his first year at university, she had turned out to be very important in his life, as she had helped him out whenever he needed. Then, suddenly, his life changed so dramatically, and in a way that was excruciatingly painful. What he had feared most came to pass. She became unavailable and short with him. Worse than that, he caught her walking down the campus of the university with another guy. When she caught sight of him, she held the young man's hand, telling him in a way that it was over between them. That cruel rejection that did hurt him went beyond emotional pain; it did inflict damage to his psychological well-being. That awful ostracism just reminded him of past rejection experiences that continued to irritate and cause him bitter resentment.

Feeling destabilised and disconnected did add to his emotional suffering, and impelled him in a last-ditch attempt to reach out to her. So, to get through this miserable situation, he decided to understand why she had decided to break up with him. Her saying she was just a friend was really good after all because being in the friend zone was much better than being far apart from each other.

That evening right after the tax course, Sadij approached Valerie to speak to her with the intent of knowing why she had suddenly decided to walk away from him.

As soon as he was right in front of her, he became speechless and kept staring at her eyes lovingly, more directly, and for a long time; it seemed as if he wanted to be completely present with her. He was so unexpectedly overtaken by a blend of euphoria, pleasure and nervous excitement that he had forgotten the purpose of this meeting. A few minutes later, he came to himself and resumed acting as he normally did.

He greeted her saying, *'How's it been?'*

'Been getting by,' she answered, looking a bit embarrassed.

Sadij wanted to know why Valerie was trying to avoid him lately, he then said, *'Long time no see!'*

Valerie explained that she had been keeping herself busy. *'At the moment, I'm swamped.'*

He then invited her for coffee, saying, *'Shall we go get coffee? Do you have any time?'*

She immediately declined his offer, saying, *'Honestly, I don't have a moment to spare.'*

But Sadij was determined to talk to her. *'Listen. Valerie, shall we shoot the breeze? 'Cause there's something I just need to talk to you about.'*

Valerie was in no mood to chat and swiftly said, *'Shall we put it off until a later time, 'cause I'm all out of time. I'll have to say good-bye now.'*

Sadij seemed to be unwilling to yield an inch, and answered in an earnest tone, *'I'm afraid, this is very important, it can't wait.'*

She became restless, nervous, and acted like a cat on hot bricks; she was shifting from one foot to the other, and finally said in a shrill voice, *'Cut to the chase. And give it to me straight, 'cause I don't have time to breathe.'*

He then requested her to go to a nearby coffee shop, which she turned down categorically, saying, *'Out with it! Here and now. Right?'*

Sadij took a deep breath and said, *'You know we've been together for almost a year now. I honestly enjoy your company. Whatever you do and wherever you are, I find myself constantly thinking about you. I don't think I'll be able to ever get you out of my mind.'*

Valerie was taken aback by Sadij's avowal of love to her, and butted him in, *'Do you have bats in your belfry? We're just friends.'*

He requested her to keep calm. *'Please, don't have a conniption. Will you just allow me to lay it on the line, 'cause this is something that's been tormenting me for a while, and I think the time has come to do away with the anguish I feel inside.'*

The look on her face showed she was not in the least enjoying what Sadij was saying. She brought her lips into her mouth, for the words that came out of Sadij's mouth caused her jaw to drop; she then moved her eyebrows upwards.

Sadij entreated her, *'Please, don't raise your eyebrows at me like that! I swear I'm ready to cancel any plans just to be with you. Nothing compares to you. I always find myself very blithe whenever I think about you. Whenever you go home, I find myself longing to spend time with you.'*

Then, she kindly requested him to hearken to her. *'Now that I've given you the chance to say your piece, I guess I have the right to tell you how I feel. Right?'* Sadij nodded in assent. *'The problem with you guys is you often misinterpret female friendliness as love. So how can I know that you've fallen for me completely while the only thing I want most is to be friends with you? I just don't want something romantic. So, let me just put my cards on the table. Never and ever delude yourself with the pious hope that I'll one day feel about you the way you feel about me. You will find someone that will feel about you that way. Let me be clear with you from the start that I'm not looking for a romantic relationship at the moment. Studies are my top priority, and I have never induced you to caress the hope of considering me more than a friend.'*

To clear the air and ward off any potential misunderstanding in the future, she said, *'Listen, Sadij. You're a good friend, and I enjoy spending time with you, but I'm just not interested in you the way you're interested in me. I just want to make this clear.'*

It all happened out of the blue, for Sadij was completely stunned to hear what Valerie had just revealed about her real feelings towards him; he was just kind of reeling from the shock of being rejected by the most beloved one.

It took Sadij a few minutes to realise what had happened; he finally found his voice and said, *'You can't believe how sorry I am. It's all my fault. I should have restrained myself from getting a bit carried away by my emotions. I should have asked you first. Please pretend I didn't say anything. I promise it will never happen again. Okay?'* She agreed and left in a hurry.

Chapter 12

Sadij had finally made the shocking realisation about the fact that he found himself in the throes of a strong and immature attachment to a girl that didn't love him back. He was wondering about whether he should stop pursuing or keep pushing forward. As customary, in difficult moments Sadij withdrew into himself and tried to give thorough and deep consideration to how to break free from the fetters of an impossible relationship.

He was sitting in his room, meditating. *Unrequited love is a hackneyed thing that most people experience in their lives. So, it's no use being depressed or sad, because I'm not alone. But do I have to remain emotionally bound to a girl who raised red flags when I confessed to my inability and unwillingness to walk away from her?* Every time he tried to reason, his heart kept messing with his head, causing him to look and listen for what he was hoping to see and hear from his unavailable Valerie.

However, the time had come to face the fact that the girl was not at all in love with him. All that Sadij needed was an ounce of courage to sever ties with Valerie, but that valiance was at the moment very hard to come by, for he was entrapped in that stupefying and inebriant dope of a romantic obsession.

His romantic and intractable infatuation with Valerie started making him do some things that were so much out of character that they amazed even him. To make sure that she hadn't been dating someone else behind his back, he went about in a sneaking way stalking her. He found himself doing things that were inconsistent with his real self.

It was on one April morning, Sadij and Valerie were sitting in the library leafing through some references. When Valerie ran to the restroom, Sadij grabbed her cell phone, swiftly read all the messages and checked all incoming and outgoing calls while casting glances at the restroom facilities adjacent to the library.

Sadij said to himself, *'I'm not like that. I will check very quickly and if I don't find anything, it will be the last time.'* Before he had time to go through all the text messages stored in her SMS inbox, out of the washroom stepped Valerie, who caught Sadij in the act of nervously touching her mobile.

As soon as his eyes met hers, his face turned red from embarrassment. Whereupon, Valerie flew into a rage, got aggressive and yelled at him.

'Leave that fucking phone right now!' Her voice was so loud that it distracted all the students present in the library and prevented them from concentrating on their work.

Sadij tried to stay calm, maintaining a poker face and calmly said, *'Why? Do you have something to hide?'*

She persisted in scolding him, *'I said, put that damned phone down and never touch it. Do you know what? This is called invading and prying into people's privacy. You've crossed the line, and you had better go and see a shrink.'*

Valerie felt violated and disappointed. By snooping through Valerie's phone, Sadij had entered into a broken trust phase. His mistrust established a pattern of behaviour that sprang from the various deceits he had experienced in the past. But Valerie wasn't at all interested in finding out the source of Sadij's mistrust. Instead of talking it through calmly, she lost her temper, freaked out on him and left the library.

Chapter 13

Valerie flipped out, obviously distraught by the mere thought of having her undeniable right to privacy and personal space being encroached upon by a person she had long put on a pedestal; she was utterly mistaken about Sadij, he wasn't as trustworthy as she had thought. She, therefore, decided to drop in on Mathilde, a close friend of hers, to spill her guts, because she was desperately in need of someone to speak truthfully to and share all that had happened in the library that morning. The emotion of sadness she felt as a result of disappointment was particularly so profound that it had decreased her confidence in first impressions.

She set about confiding in her alter ego. *'I'm at a loss for words, to be frank with you.'*

Mathilde, in an attempt to calm her down, said, *'Keep your shirt on. Tell me what happened. Just take things one day at a time.'*

Valerie pulled herself together and related every bit of the incident in the library down to the smallest details. *'It's all my fault. I shouldn't have trusted him. How silly of me!'*

Mathilde interrupted her, saying, *'Come on, put a cork in it. Most guys are naturally curious about things. Don't lose your temper and freak out like that. A few days ago, Laurent told me that he caught his girlfriend, Maya, in the act of looking at his private texts, emails, Snapchats, Facebook images, and didn't flip out.'*

Valerie, still irritated, replied, *'It's easy for you to tell me not to lose my temper. Put yourself in my shoes and tell me what you would have done, Mat! It isn't as easy as you're making it seem.'*

Mathilde, in an attempt to defuse her friend's anger, refocused Valerie's attention, saying calmly, *'Valerie, hang on a second. Let me make sure I understand you. You're saying, one, you outright caught Sadij in the act of snooping on you; two, when you asked him to leave your phone, he said you perhaps had something to hide. Right?'*

Valerie nodded to indicate she was following Mathilde's feedback. Maintaining a neutral face and a neutral voice, Mathilde proceeded with expressing her opinion, *'If I were you, I wouldn't flip out in the first place. Instead, find out the root cause of Sadij's mistrust. If you're still interested in him, try to see whether he has been deceived before. You know that snooping through someone's phone shows insecurity. Do have a serious conversation with him to prevent it from happening again. Then, you may decide whether or not you want to remain in the relationship. After all, it's up to you to decide whether you could hang with someone that cannot have faith in you.'*

While Mathilde was speaking, Valerie was watching the movement of her friend's hands very closely and paying close heed to her advice. Mathilde's tone of voice turned into impartiality. *'May I ask you a question?'* she asked.

'Of course,' replied Valerie, who looked less upset than before.

Mathilde, looking her friend straight in the eyes, asked in a more earnest note, *'Could you be with someone that doesn't trust you?'*

'Are you nuts? Of course not,' she swiftly answered.
'So, if you can't put up with someone that can't put his trust in you, you had better move on. Otherwise, you will get your ass kicked very often, because if this snooping of his happens again and again, this establishes a pattern of behaviour that can never be remedied, and you're likely to suffer as a result. This behaviour is toxic.'

Upon hearing this, Valerie looked worried and started having negative thoughts and feelings about Sadij; she then asked Mathilde to make her point a bit clearer. *'Get to the point. What are you trying to say?'*

Mathilde gave it to her straight, *'Let me repeat myself. If Sadij snoops on you again, it means he's sick and is trying to control you. It is your life that is at stake... I mean you deserve to live free and happy. You had better consider leaving sooner rather than later.'*

Valerie agreed, saying, *'So it seems.'*

After the exhaustive discussion she had had with her friend, Valerie realised that snooping on a friend was a terrible and atrocious thing to do and that in a healthy friendship, both parties should trust each other unconditionally. At last, she thanked her friend for her precious advice and said goodbye to each other.

Chapter 14

It was really hard for Sadij to feel disappointed by the girl he had cherished in his innermost heart. Suddenly, Sadij's life changed dramatically, for Valerie had gone missing both physically and emotionally. Dejected and almost without hope, he was on a downer as he vehemently resented Valerie's lack of attention to him. He had never longed for things to turn out that way. How he wished things could be the way they had once been. But the harm was already done. Valerie's unavailability and indifference did add to his stress as he tried to come to terms with this swift and unwanted change in his life.

He ruefully looked back upon the moments he had spent in Valerie's company; he remembered how they both used to study together. He tried to adjust to this change in his life, but to no avail. He then started reproaching himself for what had come to pass that Friday at his grandmother's. Had he known that the encounter between Valerie and Mrs Moukafiha would turn sour, he wouldn't have invited the former. But what was done couldn't be undone. The loss of Valerie just contributed to feeding Sadij's fear, for he had become more afraid than ever before of having no friends at all in the future.

The negative self-talk started rearing its ugly head. *It's all my fault. What do I expect? First, she was hurt in her dignity and pride by a narrow-minded woman. How could she put up with it? I don't deserve her, because I'm not a reliable person. I ought to have stuck my neck out for her. How stupid of me not to have taken sides against my grandmother. Second, I spied on her phone, which is a breach of privacy, I must admit; it simply means I don't trust her.*

Sadij couldn't manage to bring himself to accept that change in a relationship was an ineluctable part of life, which did set him up for gratuitous distress and anguish. And getting angry about what transpired was to Sadij just like hitting his head against the wall, for anger came right back at him like a boomerang. Because his relationship with Valerie changed in a way that wasn't to his liking, his anger got more intense. He was mistaken to think that his relationship with Valerie would always remain the same. He spent the whole day engaging in self-blame. He also started questioning the validity of the feelings he had been fostering for Valerie.

All of a sudden, a gloomy aura of pessimism pervaded his whole being. *Not getting what I want in this life is my inevitable fate. I was born to suffer. How I wish I were dead. I'm cursed. I'm not cut out for having friends in life. It runs in our family. We're the wrong breed for dating and getting married. There isn't a single day that passes by without one of my wishes and desires going fulfilled. How can I ever forgive myself for having let the chance of a lifetime slip through my fingers?'*

Unable to stand being rejected, he engaged in finding faults in himself, lamenting all his shortcomings and beating himself to a pulp. It was really hard for Sadij to prevent the psychological fallouts that occurred in the aftermath of his breaking up with Valerie. To allay the excruciatingly emotional pain that Valerie's rejection of him had brought about, he called on his friend, Jaaba.

The latter was taking up residence in a tiny studio apartment in the fifteenth district of Paris. It was a very small space, but thanks to Jaaba's knack for decoration, he had managed to make the most of that tiny studio apartment. Decorating his studio required Jaaba's inventive imagination, a step-by-step conception and modifications, but the end was well worth the time and effort expended. He had managed to fit the living room, the kitchen and bedroom into one room and still had room to breathe. Though the studio was very small, Jaaba had brought in standout elements by adding bold touches here and there; on the right side of the entry, there was an eye-catching and breath-taking picture of Niagara Falls. He had furnished his studio with pieces that folded away when not in use.

For instance, he had a Murphy bed that folded and swung to store vertically against the wall; close to the American kitchenette, there was a drop-leaf dining table that could become a dining area when in use. Jaaba was a very ingenious home designer, for he had created a division between his sleeping area and the rest of the space with folding screens and bookcases. He rented this very small studio for an affordable price. Sadij was fascinated by this true cocoon, which put a bug in his ear about getting a similar cosy space for himself – a space where he could feel free, at home, without feeling accountable to anyone.

Jaaba, who was making coffee, launched the conversation, *'So, pal, what is it that is so important that you want to talk to me about?'*

Without speaking in circles, Sadij spared his friend nothing, and rounded off his narrative of the stressful incident with self-blame. *'I guess I screwed everything up this time.'*

Jaaba looked a bit surprised and requested his friend to get to the point. *'Get to the heart of the matter. Tell me what happened.'*

He then recounted all the details of the incident that took place in the library and explained that it was out of fear that she might be dating someone else that he felt compelled to snoop on her phone.

Upon hearing about Sadij's prying into the private space of Valerie, Jaaba expressed his disapproval. *'If you want my opinion, you don't have a leg to stand on, because the moment you've snooped, you've become untrustworthy. If I were you and had a good reason to believe that my friend was being kind of shady, I would talk to her directly. One thing you need to know is women do like men that are not insecure. And by prying into her private affairs, you're kind of turning her off. If you trust Valerie, why check her phone?'*

Sadij's insecurity drove a toxic wedge between him and Valerie. Looking helpless and desperate, he was ready to hold onto any tiny flicker of hope coming from his pal.

Finally, Jaaba, feeling dejected and down, stood up, made for the window that looked out on a nearby park, and said, *'Can I bend your ear a second?'*

Sadij, heaving a deep sigh of regret, answered, *'I'm all ears.'*

'Well, I advise you to first get rid of your insecurities.'

'How?' inquired Sadij.

'Very simple. Try to build your self-esteem. And then find out the root cause of your insecurity.'

Sadij seemed to be offended and responded swiftly, *'What do you mean? I have no idea what you're talking about.'*

Jaaba sat down on the couch and resumed his explanation, *'The point is you need to dig deep and think back to what's wreaking havoc on your confidence. Is it something that has to do with your mum? I don't know. I'm just conjecturing from experience. Look, there's nothing wrong with being jealous. But when jealousy oversteps its bounds, a relationship is bound to founder.'*

While Jaaba was talking, Sadij was listening with rapt attention. Sadij did allow jealousy to sink its teeth too deep in his relationship with Valerie that it took a toll on Valerie. Before Jaaba put the lid on the pointers he was imparting to his close friend, he quickly added, *'I hope you won't take what I'm going to tell you to heart. But I think you need to give Valerie some space. I mean if you don't stop being on her ass all the time, she will feel smothered and attacked, and you will lose her for good. Dig?'*

Sadij nodded in assent. Jaaba stood and walked over to the window again, staring out as if he was waiting for someone to show up. Sadij asked, *'Are you expecting someone? I'll leave if I bother you, you know.'*

Jaaba reacted very swiftly, *'I got a date with a girl.'* He then cast a glance at his wrist-watch and said, *'It won't be long before she turns up.'*

Sadij was curious to know who that girl was and asked, *'The same girl you go out with?'*

Jaaba, looking anxious, expressed his disagreement. *'Absolutely not! I have lately succeeded in getting that pretty blonde Danish girl that has a curvaceous figure, and who is much too intelligent and pretty to be dating the likes of me. I have invited her to my studio for a Moroccan tea.'*

Sadij understood that his friend wanted to be on his own; he then thanked him for his precious tips and left in a hurry.

Chapter 15

Sadij was highly originative and not suited to continue living under his grandmother's roof. So far, he hadn't managed to impose his will and establish his identity after a long and vain battle to stand his ground in his family. Now that he was pursuing his graduate studies at the Paris Diderot University, he felt that it was tremendously important for him to evolve his own authentic sense of self and sever the umbilical cord with Mrs Moukafiha. He realised that when under his grandmother's influence, his sense of self-worth kept crumbling; that desire to have the ability to take a stand and say no for just once started to take hold of him.

Contemplating the issue from all sides, it finally dawned upon him that if he were away from her, and not looking at himself through her eyes, he could be more confident, more productive, more independent and obviously on track in his personal and professional development. He remembered how he had been very lugubrious and completely unsure of himself; he could also recollect how his younger brother had always been the family star, and how everything he would do was seen as a feat; he remembered with resentment that his mother had never radiated with pride in whatever he did.

He decided to stop acting like an emotionally weak child, confront his grandmother and explain to her that it was high time he threw that albatross around his neck; he was excited to tell her without trepidation this time that he was no longer willing to toe the line, obey and cower so as not to receive her displeasure. Mrs Moukafiha would no longer have the chance to stifle her grandson's attempt at creating his identity. That visit that he had paid to his friend, Jaaba, turned out to be the real trigger. He was fascinated by the easiness with which his friend made independent decisions without unhealthily taking into consideration the opinion of his parents.

Sadij was overly in need of pleasing his grandmother because he feared that if he didn't, then she would abandon him. This time, he made a complete volte-face on his stance concerning his relationship with his grandmother. He was determined more than ever to become a full-fledged adult, emotionally and physically independent of his grandmother.

Tonight, he was going to spill the beans in a very respectful way. The sooner he confronted her, the better he would feel, though he was concerned about how she would respond. He was determined to schedule a meeting with her instead of broaching the topic with her through a sudden and unexpected conversation. He had chosen an appropriate time and place where he could be more comfortable and planned what he wanted to say beforehand. As Mrs Moukafiha was fond of chocolate ice cream, it occurred to Sadij that it would be a bright idea if he could just take her for a walk on a panoramic tour of Montmartre Sacré-Cœur basilica. Montmartre was a couple of kilometres north of Paris city centre.

To get to it, Sadij and his grandmother took the funicular railway that ran up the west side of the park area to in front of Sacre-Cœur Basilica. Mrs Moukafiha enjoyed seeing many artists that congregated in that very beautiful and quiet place to draw the visitors that rushed to this very famous touristic site in Paris. She was delighted to see various cafés, bars and restaurants frequented mainly by tourists coming from different parts of the world.

After their visit to Montmartre, they walked over to Berthillon, a famous ice cream shop in Paris. The line to buy ice cream was long, but they found it well worth the wait. Sadij ordered a single scoop of the salted caramel ice cream for himself, while Mrs Moukafiha ordered her favourite dark chocolate ice cream.

While eating their ice creams, Mrs Moukafiha asked Sadij, *'You said you wanted to talk to me about something. I'm listening, dearest one.'*

Sadij was a bit embarrassed, because Mrs Moukafiha had pulled him up short; he didn't see it coming…

He started stammering. *'Yea… sure… I just want to tell you that it takes time and money to shuttle between Champigny and Diderot University, and I think that it would be advisable for me to rent a very small studio or a maid's room and settle in there.'*

The gist of Sadij's words sparked resentful anger in Mrs Moukafiha; they cut straight to her heart, like a knife twisted and turned, *'Are you telling me that you're leaving me, and you don't want to see me any more?'*

When Sadij's turn to talk came, he spoke slowly, calmly, lowering his vocal tone, *'Of course not. You mean the world to me. The point is, I want to focus on my future career. I mean, I have to find ways to make money… I just don't want to be at the mercy of anyone. I just don't want you to misinterpret my words. I just want to be a man. I just turned twenty-one years old, and it's high time I started to fend for myself. You've always been there for me. This I will never forget. I would love to return all the favours you gave me. You've proved to be the first compass by which I've oriented myself in this world. You don't have to think that it does make me happy to live apart from you.'*

Tears welled in Mrs Moukafiha's eyes, as Sadij was laying bare his intention of severing the ties that had been binding both of them.

'Don't worry, Grandma, everything will be just fine. I'm a ripe man. All I want is to form a new and independent life for myself away from the precious help that you've been providing me with all along. Rest assured that we will be seeing each other very often.'

Mrs Moukafiha approached to give him a tight hug. She got used to Sadij and knew that getting estranged from him would undoubtedly take a serious toll on the happiness and joy she used to feel in his company. Sadij was acutely aware of the fact that this separation would destabilise his grandmother and leave her feeling lost, but he felt that the time had come to embrace his would-be new-found freedom. All of a sudden, Mrs Moukafiha who once held an important place in Sadij's life had become just a shade.

Sadij realised that he had to go against the grain of his family because of the toxic behaviour of both his mother and his grandmother; the emotional and mental abuses that he had suffered while living with his mother and stepfather did make the cut necessary. The incongruity of mentality and expectations had brought about a wellspring of dashing hopes and hurt feelings that were hard to heal. Finally, Mrs Moukafiha resigned herself to the fact that Sadij had to pack up and leave.

PART III

Chapter 1

Looking for a studio to rent in Paris wasn't as easy as Sadij had expected; it was his first time searching for a studio in Paris. Before he put his pen to paper and signed a lease, he had had to first go to the CROUS of Paris, a public institution whose mission was to promote the improvement of the living conditions of the students of the Paris Academy through the management of student social assistance, student housing, university catering and the reception of international students.

At the entrance of this student service office, Sadij was dazzled by the numerous housing ads that were posted on a huge display panel. He then took a pen out of his pocket and started scrawling down the ads that appeared to be very interesting, and made some calls to arrange to meet the landlords to make sure whether he could afford to move in one of those small studios and live there.

Eventually, he managed to make an appointment with a Jewish landlady, taking up residence in Square Moncey in the ninth district of Paris. That sturdy lady owned a very small studio located in the same street. He met her on the same day. The owner of the studio was living in a very distinctive upscale building whose design and architecture were very modern. When Sadij arrived, he found the lady waiting for him at the entrance of the building. After introductions had been made, she took him to visit the studio she was willing to let. The landlady's face was impassive and showed no emotion; she was wearing a sumptuous knee-length fur coat that showed her status and wealth. Under that very expensive fur coat, there was a button-through dress that had buttons that went from the top to the bottom. That loose-fitting and conservative outfit she was wearing gave her an aura of solemnity and gravity. She had long straight blonde hair and a facial tic when she was laying down her conditions to Sadij; with a furrowed brow and upper lip curled into a scowl, she dotted the i's and crossed the t's.

'First of all, you need to know, young man, that pets aren't allowed. Second, there's a deposit to hold the rental property before you move in, as there were some other students that have already visited the studio this morning. So, if you're interested, then you have to pay a deposit of five per cent of the total rent. If ever you change your mind, the deposit is non-refundable. Remember the rule. First come, first served. This is exactly what I had told the other potential tenants.'

Sadij was afraid that he might run the risk of squandering this rare opportunity to achieve his goals at a relatively low cost. He agreed with the terms of the lease with alacrity and took a note of fifty francs out of his pocket to provide reassurance that he was serious about renting the studio.

The landlady took the money and said, *'One last final condition before finalising the rental contract, I would like to draw your attention to the fact that I'm letting this studio in a good, habitable condition. So, if there are any chips in the paint or cracks in the window, it will be at your own expense. Right?'*

Sadij showed no objection. He was very fortunate because he had no security deposit to pay. The deal was done, Sadij took leave of the landlady and went away.

Chapter 2

Like many students in the capital of France, Sadij's schedule was consumed by more classes and assignments. Now, he spent almost the same amount of time working as a dishwasher in Pub St. Germain des Près. He worked there five days a week to make both ends meet and cover housing and other living costs. As Sadij wasn't much of a talker, he worked very diligently and minded his own business; he didn't grumble about the bad working conditions he was suffering from. For him to have a job at that very moment was a godsent opportunity. He worked the night shift to show up on campus for morning classes.

Sometimes, he couldn't help falling asleep during the lectures because of overwork. He was the backbone of the pub, for the bussers, waiters, maître d'hôtels largely depended on him. One Saturday night, the tavern was packed to the rafters, and everyone was up to their ears in work. The owner of the pub, Mr Dauvois, flew into a temper because he found a lipstick stain on a wine glass.

So, he gave Sadij a fierce scolding. *'Qu'est ce que c'est que ce travail d'arabe?'*, alluding and in front of some waiters to the fact that Sadij bungled his work. The poor chap felt stigmatised, and within that period that he had been working in that damned tavern that pejorative expression had stuck with him. Some racist maîtres d'hôtel would call him *"bougnoule"* meaning "a wog", other waiters would flip him off for no obvious reason. He knew that these kinds of disparaging and discriminatory remarks were very common in Paris, even if they were only made by certain people. Humiliating and degrading Sadij went too far.

One night, while he was collecting used utensils from the dining area, a customer repulsively puked his dinner up. Immediately, Sadij was summoned to clean up the mess. His work was not restricted to washing dishes and mopping the floor; he, after loading and unloading the dishwasher appliance, had to store clean items and equipment properly and go down to the basement to handwash large pots and other wooden cutting boards. And before clocking out, he had to take out the trash. To wash away the daily humiliation he was exposed to, he would weep while taking a shower to conceal his vulnerability from his co-workers. What a stoic personality that young man enjoyed! Despite all the hardships he faced, he kept a stiff upper lip.

Upon reaching his new dwelling place, Sadij took the stairs rather than the lift, as he had been instructed to do by the landlady when he signed the lease. She had made it clear from the outset that the elevator was exclusively reserved for property owners. So, poor Sadij, after a long, tiring night at work, had to climb the stairs up to the sixth floor. Jaded and completely tired, he would stop for a breath on the third floor to recharge his batteries. As soon as he got to the sixth floor, he would sometimes set the alarm clock for the following night shift and throw himself down on the bed. However, when he had class, he would stop for a coffee at Le Relais Odéon, and then walked to the university hastily and frantically.

Whenever assignments kept rolling in, he knew how to

get himself in the right work mood. On his days off, he would hit the library to research his end-term paper. His afternoons were spent reading stuff he was interested in. Working a full-time job was a daunting undertaking, but Sadij had managed to handle the issue thanks to a good level of planning and prioritisation. Studying while working had given Sadij the confidence he needed, as he, at last, felt financially independent. At the beginning of every semester, he obtained all his syllabi, took note of all exam schedules, wrote them down together with the deadlines for the submission of some papers. He wasn't the kind of guy that would waste his time, for he used the free time he had constructively; while commuting almost every day to his work by subway, he would read a book, a newspaper article or he would go over the notes he had taken the day before.

Working like a dog in the pub during the nights and studying hard during the daytime had ineluctably caused Sadij to stress out now and then. To manage this stress in a very positive way, he resorted to jogging. Sometimes, he would go for a walk. These physical activities proved to be efficient stress relievers, for they had boosted Sadij's concentration and cognitive levels. He successfully passed the final exam, and got a bachelor's degree in economic sciences. Now, he would be able to apply for a job that required mental rather than physical stamina. He was finally hired as a data entry clerk by DHL in Courbevoie. It was a part-time job, and he wouldn't have to bust his hump to save money for a rainy day. He worked less and earned more.

Here, he was treated with dignity and respect; the workplace was good and all co-workers were willing to help; the manager was nice, and gave all employees equal attention.

It was an amazing work experience. Sadij had acquired proficient typing skills, good customer service, and administrative skills. Most employees working at DHL went on vacation in the summer. The management was desperately in need of hands; so the boss offered Sadij a full-time job with some fringe benefits, such as meal vouchers. He was also assigned a company car to support his transportation needs for the job. That was something Sadij had never dreamt of.

Chapter 3

During one of his frequent visits to his grandmother, Sadij learned that his mother, Makiera, was having problems with her husband, Ablah. The former felt being financially put upon. Mrs Moukafiha was resolved to put her grandson wise to the latest developments in his mother's asymmetric relationship with Ablah.

Mrs Moukafiha made a coughing sound while adjusting her headscarf, and said, *'I think you have the right to know all about the kinds of problems your mother is having right now; besides, I believe that washing one's dirty linen should be carried out at home.'*

Sadij was listening with rapt attention, weighing every single word coming out of his grandmother's mouth.

The old woman proceeded with her speech, *'Ablah has turned out to be a liar, impostor, crook and a freeloader. He refused to split the rent with your mother and stopped providing for his family. She just got a huge gas and electricity bill that he hasn't paid for the past three months. And every time she told him about it, he kept saying that he would do it. He even used her car almost every day, while she had to go to work by bus. To crown it all, when she is not around, he brings his friends home to create mayhem all over the place. Oh, yeah... yesterday, she told me that when she came home from work, every light in every room was on. What is exasperating in all of this is that he doesn't seem to care that she is the one that's paying the bills.'*

Sadij, unable to stand the unfair treatment his mother was receiving at the hands of that rascal, hit the table with his fist so violently that two tea glasses fell onto the floor, splashing the Turkish carpet that Mrs Moukafiha had brought as a token of remembrance from her trip to Istanbul.

Mrs Moukafiha was dumbfounded by Sadij's reaction. *'Relax, Take it easy. All I'm doing is establishing the facts, you don't have to bite my head off because you're upset.'*

He then apologised, *'I'm very sorry. I lost my temper. I didn't mean to snap your head off.'* He pulled himself together, took slow, deep breaths from his nose and exhaled out of his mouth for some minutes. He then resumed his speech, *'I'm so furious. I've never been so mad in my life. I just don't know what to say. There's a hammering inside my head.'*

She asked him to relax, *'Mellow out, my boy. All this is her fault. She ought to have done something about it a long time ago. Besides, she's really stupid because the scoundrel has slyly managed to make her believe that he loves her and that she's the woman of his dreams. He's a smooth-talker.'*

Sadij said, *'I don't want to interrupt you, but I knew from the very beginning that he was a wily old fox. He's loving her for all the freeloading, I guess. She's reduced herself to a cheap hotel in Paris. She can't go on living like this. I think she's got to the point where she has to expel him from the house.'*

Mrs Moukafiha looked at him rather askance when Sadij came up with this suggestion of his. She then expressed her disapproval, *'Listen, my son, she has four small kids now, her husband is what he is and isn't going to change.'*

Sadij disagreed completely, *'Oh, that's just horse feathers, and you know it. If a glass is broken, you can't fix it. I'm unsure about what to expect and how to pick up the pieces. After all, marriages are not death sentences.'*

Mrs Moukafiha beside herself with anger shouted out at her grandson, *'She should stay with her husband for the kids.'*

Upon hearing this, Sadij started seething with rage. *'Do you want her children to grow up in a loveless home where their father doesn't have an ounce of respect for their mother? Your daughter's happiness has no price.'*

'I know, but your mother cannot leave the marriage because she still loves that villain.'

Sadij realised that his mother, Makiera, wasn't actually living her life, she was just coping and plugging along. But at the same time, he didn't want his brothers to experience the same ordeals he had been through; he didn't want to see them being shunted from one home to the next either.

Mrs Moukafiha grabbed Sadij's wrist and begged him not to meddle with his mother's relationship issues.

'It's not that easy for a woman to be divorced. Makiera is going to suffer because she will have to encounter stigma wherever she goes. She will have to face up to interpersonal sanctions by individuals with whom she interacts. She's going to run the risk of being excluded from social interaction. I'm a woman and I know what it's like to be divorced. Mrs Anissa's divorced daughter told me that she, out of jealousy, was rejected by her married friends, because they believed that her presence destabilised their marriages.'

Sadij disapproved of Mrs Moukafiha's line of reasoning; he intervened and told his grandmother, *'We have to stand by her and my brothers, and provide all sorts of material and emotional support to them. Besides, we're not living in a traditional society where women lack the courage to ask for a divorce.'*

Mrs Moukafiha reacted very quickly. *'You're talking*

nonsense, dear. For the children's sake, I'll do whatever it may take to save her failing marriage to Ablah. Promise me that you will stay away from this domestic dispute!'

Sadij reassured his grandmother that he would by no means poke his nose into his mother's private life, cast a glance at his wristwatch, sprang to his feet and said, *'Look at the time. I really must go. We will continue this another time.'*

Chapter 4

Although Makiera was a bit licentious around the edges and open-minded, at no time was she able to seek a divorce, because she was brought up in a traditional environment where women did not dare to ask for a divorce and violate the social norms they were reared in. For her mother, Mrs Moukafiha, it behoved Makiera to meekly perform the role of the wife and the mother.

Furthermore, to all Maghribian emigrants living in the vicinity of Bois l'Abbé, to divorce was the most abominable thing a woman could do. Mrs Moukafiha tried to prevent her daughter from resorting to divorce as a first solution. They both got together to discuss the issue. Makiera had run out of patience and was on pins and needles.

'I'm fed up with being always confined to the typical role of a submissive wife that does all household chores and raises her children. Enough is enough.'

Mrs Moukafiha, feeling very anxious about her daughter's future, said, *'Cut to the chase. I don't see what you're getting at.'*

At the end of her tether, Makiera cried out, *'This is more than I can take. Mum. My frustration is getting bigger and bigger day after day. I have a small car and own a nice flat; I work very hard, and sometimes till late hours. He's been staying with me for more than ten years now. He scarcely uses his car. He uses mine almost every day. It has never occurred to him to help me with paying the household bills.'*

Mrs Moukafiha tried to calm her daughter down. *'Simmer down... because if you don't, you will send yourself to an early grave.'*

Makiera, beside herself with ire, said, *'I'm already dead, can't you see? Oh, Mum, I'm sick of lying; my relationship with him has been ending for a long time. I've been suffering in silence and didn't want to bother you with my problems. But now it's the last straw.'*

Mrs Moukafiha remained unyielding and continued to speak with a resolute voice, *'Don't you know that divorced women are looked down up, and are relegated to a very low position in society?'*

Makiera started giggling and scoffing at her mother, *'How can you be so stupid, Mum? You can't be serious. We're in France... and unlike Morocco where poor divorced women occupy a third space in society and are regarded as chattels, here in France, those women are named single mothers and if you allow me, they do enjoy all their rights to the full. Furthermore, the French culture doesn't encourage stereotypes in gender roles. To jog your memory a little bit about this, Nassima's husband often takes care of the kids and caters for the family while Nassima is on a business trip.'*

Mrs Moukafiha rolled her eyes while saying, *'I wonder if Ablah is going to look after the kids when you're working overtime.'*

Makiera shook her head back and forth and said, *'Go ahead, laugh yourself sick. Of course, he will change Ashraf's diapers when hell freezes over. Listen, Mum! Gone are the days when a woman's role was restricted to performing household chores and taking care of kids. Today, in a relationship, both partners stand united and equal in their contributions to themselves and each other. In my couple, I'm giving more than I take, and this is getting on my nerves. I just can't see the worth and the value that he's bringing to my life. I can't put up with his taking advantage of me, and this has got to stop.'*

No longer able to follow her daughter, Mrs Moukafiha tried to keep Makiera in the picture, *'You just don't care about what our neighbours will say. They will say that you're the kind of woman that likes to go out constantly and have fun with friends, neglecting her home and her children.'*

Makiera continued to stand up to her mother, *'I don't care a hang about what people may say. People just keep gossiping no matter what. If I don't value myself, he'll never give me my due. It's all my fault because I have always put my own needs on the back-burner for him.'*

Mrs Moukafiha could not understand her daughter, and kept scratching her chin, *'Have you flipped your lid, you idiot? You just don't wake up one day and decide to let Ablah take advantage of you? You've always let his needs and desires come first, and if there's someone to blame, it's you. Just think about your children. They will be teased by their classmates because of their parents' divorce. Can't you see the emotional pain they will have to feel when they find themselves unable to choose which of their parents they're going to spend their birthdays and holidays with?'*

Makiera straightened her arms out to the sides and turned the palms up, moving them only a little left and right in keeping with the rhythm of her voice. She suddenly grew tired of laying it on the line, stood up and said, *'It's no use explaining to you the anguish I'm going through. I had better go.'*

She slammed the door shut and left.

Chapter 5

It was a Tuesday morning, and Makiera got up early as Ablah had told her the day before to wake him up for an early morning trip for his work. She was preparing breakfast in the kitchen, holding her nine-month-old baby with only one hand while making breakfast with the other. He seemed to be in a great hurry and kept pacing back and forth in the hallway that led to the kitchen like a sentry rubbing his hands together, and now and then taking a peek at his wife to see if breakfast was ready. Makiera was doing her utmost to serve breakfast to her husband without further delay, when all of a sudden, Ablah hauled off, smacked Makiera across her face and yelled at her, *'When am I going to have that damned breakfast, you fucking slut?'*

That slap was so violent that Makiera's glasses flew off her face, bending the frame and leaving a swollen bruise on her cheekbone. She was stunned, for she had never known this kind of physical abuse before.

'What did you that for?' she asked.

'You don't know? Well, you deserve to be flogged to death, you scarlet woman; I'm late because of you.'

'Mind what you're saying. You had better weigh your words!'

'And if I don't, what are you going to do?'

'I'm not a punching bag. Every time you have a problem,

you take it out on me. You're always gathering all of your frustration and putting it on me. Don't ever touch me, or…'

'Or what? Are you going to call the police, you weakling idiot?'

'I guess you have psychiatric issues, and you had better see a shrink.' The moment she uttered this, there was an avalanche of slaps that greeted her. She threatened to leave the house and call the police.

'I swear to God, if you ever touch me, you will regret it for the rest of your life. You're a ruthless bully. Can't you at least have an ounce of compassion for your baby that's crying?'

The hard-hearted husband's anger subsided and then he went out, leaving the poor Makiera sobbing and eagerly asking God to urgently punish her assaulter.

Chapter 6

Everyone in the neighbourhood of Bois l'Abbé seemed to think that Makiera was really happy in her marriage, but the reality was quite different. Ablah could charm the birds out of the trees. Makiera and Ablah did possess all the requisite ingredients to lead a blithe conjugal life; they had a charming home and plenty of money. This was how they were viewed by the neighbours. Appearances were misleading, for once that ostensibly nice and fascinating young man was at home with his wife, he became a completely different person. Makiera had to bear the brunt of his irascibility. Whenever he flew off the handle, he would become hostile and belligerent and would end up beating her to death.

One day, Ablah's aggressive behaviour had resulted in Makiera having her nose broken and her ribs cracked. She was then taken to the hospital. But when she was asked about what had happened, she said she had fallen off a ladder. The next morning, he came to her apologetic, saying that he just couldn't help himself, promising that this would never happen again. So, Makiera ended up forgiving him. Makiera found it hard to keep her being battered to death by her husband a secret because it had become a habit.

At first, she was ashamed of telling her mother about it; but at last, she decided to drop hints about the physical and emotional abuse she was the victim of to Mrs Moukafiha during the Feast of the Sacrifice, but her mother downplayed it saying that there were ups and downs in all marriages and that her daughter had to put up with it. Seeing that her mother didn't realise how frightened she was that this domestic violence might linger on, escalate and take on unwanted proportions, she decided to talk about it with her intimate friend, Sabira.

That evening, she dropped by her friend's house to take a cup of coffee with her and thereby chat about what had happened lately. After having gotten all her talking done with Sabira, the latter asked her, *'Why is he beating you? Have you done something wrong? If so, then you can adjust your behaviour, and then he won't beat you any longer.'*

Makiera explained that she had never done anything wrong to deserve to be beaten.

Sabira was not the kind of person that minced her words; therefore, she didn't want to gloss over what befell her intimate friend, and said, *'Listen to me, dear Makiera, you've got to get the hell out of dodge as quick as you can. I hate divorce, but in your case, I think it's a permanent and suitable solution to such aggressive behaviour. So, if I were you, I would pack my bags, pick up my dignity and go. You have to show him that you won't stand this behaviour any more. Once he will be by himself, he will tilt at windmills.'*

Makiera, a bit exasperated, let out a yelp. *'Come on, Sabira. The flat is mine, and if there's someone that has to leave, it's him.'*

Sabira cast a sympathetic look at her friend and said, *'I mean you certainly don't deserve what he's doing to you. A man that beats a woman is no man. He's a bully and a coward. Don't subject yourself to his abuse. And since the flat is yours, then all you have to do is to kick him out. If you're afraid that he may batter you, have your father with you to protect you.'*

Makiera didn't see eye to eye with her friend on this last suggestion and said, *'I will get my father embroiled in my problems over my dead body.'*

Sabira, determined to spare her friend any further suffering, said, *'Staying in an abusive relationship is accepting a life of anguish and suffering. My hunch is that this is only going to get worse.'* Then she asked Makiera, *'Tell me, does he abuse you emotionally?'*

This embarrassing question had, at last, made the scales fall from Makiera's eyes, and caused her to start tracking down the first time Ablah had begun abusing her emotionally. Whereupon, she poured her heart out to Sabira.

'We were living together happily for the first year, and when we had our first baby, things changed. He got into the habit of criticising anything I did; and most of the time, he made sarcastic allusions to my first marriage, insinuating that it was my fault if Taib had deserted me. Sometimes, he would put me down in front of others. In short, he had become very grumpy with me. At first, I put it down to his work stresses; I used to find excuses for his ugly behaviour. But by the time I gave birth to my second son, I just felt he hated me and I began to get depressed. Throughout the years, his behaviour got worse and worse; more criticisms, not a single attempt at having a conversation with me. I have been wondering about what has caused my husband to change into this nasty person, and it has finally dawned upon me that he was probably always like that, and he was just hiding it from me until he felt he got fed up with me.'

Feeling compassion and pity for her friend, Sabira said, *'I understand what you're saying. But your situation is a bit tricky, as it involves kids. Your children need to be removed from this unhealthy environment. You know kids learn what they see and imitate. Do you want your sons to learn that the best strategy to manage their anger is to batter their wives? Well, again if you feel you cannot do anything to change him, just kick him out.'*

Makiera, beside herself with ire, added, *'What exasperates me is that he always shows his false charming self in the presence of others. He's really a creeping hypocrite.'*

Sabira cast doubts on Ablah's faithfulness when she commented, *'Don't you think that he's maybe having an affair?'*

That unexpected revelation startled Makiera who quickly responded, *'To be true, I have no evidence for that. You may be right, who knows?'*

Sabira rubbed salt into her friend's wound when she said, *'Anyway, never trust a man that cannot manage his anger. Please hear me out, if you choose to accept his fake apologies and stay with him, be sure that this domestic violence will happen again and again and again... I just wish you a happier and better life than the shitty life you're experiencing right now.'*

She then hugged her intimate friend and added, *'You don't deserve to be treated like that. It just makes my blood boil to see that you're not happy in your marriage. If you need any help, don't hesitate to call me. You know where you can find me. Okay?'*

They kissed goodbye and parted.

Chapter 7

The episode of a husband being unable to control his anger continued. So, whenever there was an argument over petty things, Ablah would end up showering slaps on Makiera and beating her up to death. But this time, he didn't say he was sorry. She felt isolated and couldn't reach out to her family and her friends, because Ablah had managed to undermine her support systems, owing to his outward false appearance of being a nice man. The more Makiera let him get away with it, the worse he became. Not only did he stop apologising, but he began accusing her of being crazy. She asked that he treat her with more respect, but he would take no responsibility and put the blame on her.

At times, she would end up apologising to him to stop the squabble. She now realised that he didn't love her at all; she got depressed and went to a therapist and confided in him. The psychiatrist told her to convince her husband to come to some counselling. To her dismay, Ablah told her that she had gone off her chump and that it was she who ought to be seeing a shrink. Not long after that, she had a mental breakdown and was admitted to the hospital.

When her son, Sadij, heard the news, he immediately went the hospital. His mother had never had such a terrible thing before. He was shocked to learn that his mother was diagnosed with agitated depression. Had he stayed with his mother and his stepfather, he wouldn't have successfully completed his graduate studies; he was now working at Sanofi, a French multinational pharmaceutical company headquartered in Paris. Sadij was surprised when Makiera made a complete volte-face on her behaviour towards him. From a manipulative, ruthless and withholding mother that used to turn his world upside down to an ingenious, caring, and doting woman.

He had no sooner set foot in her sickroom than she jumped into her victim role and tried to make Sadij feel guilty for having forsaken her and let her down. *'Oh, my dear son, you just can't imagine how much I've been missing you. I'm very annoyed with you. It has never occurred to you to call me or drop in to see me.'*

Sadij knew that she was trying to guilt-trip him and place the finger of responsibility on him for all the anguish she was experiencing.

So, he kept quiet and refrained from twisting the knife in her aching wounds. Instead, he went off at a tangent and talked about his busy schedule. *'You know, Mother, I've been running around just like a chicken with its head cut off. I've been keeping my nose to the grindstone to make both ends meet, plus plugging away at my research paper. I swear I've been meaning to call you. I just don't want to disturb you, for I know that you're snowed under too; in addition to your work and domestic chores, you have to take care of your husband and my brothers—'*

Before he finished speaking, she had cut him off, and had gone around playing the victim, telling poor Sadij, *'I just don't know what I did to deserve this. I've done so much for all of you. And now everybody is walking out on me.'*

He was appalled to see that she denied that anything was

her fault, and tried to use her son's compassion for her advantage, which made her one of the biggest hypocrites Sadij had ever met. He couldn't give her a piece of his mind, as she was suffering from a mental breakdown, and her psychiatrist had prescribed a high dose of drugs to her.

He, therefore, apologised to her and asked, '*How can I make it up to you, Mum. Just tell me. I'm at your bidding.*'

She took him in her arms and hugged him very tightly. Then she said, '*Oh, dear son, there's nothing you can do. I'm done for. Over all the years I've been married to Ablah, I've always supported him as much as I could. I have always done everything in the house, despite my working full-time in the hospital. And I have never really minded that, though I think it would be a bright idea to get some recognition now and then for all the sacrifices I make to make our matrimonial life run smoothly. I'm getting nowt in return. Worse than that, he's beating me up for no obvious reason, and he's doing it in front of your brothers; he keeps criticising everything I do in front of your brothers. And this upsets me because I believe battering and quarrelling should not take place in front of children. So, you see the hellish life I'm leading. I'm finished.*'

She started behaving in ways that had no bearing on the imagined norms of civilised conduct. She started weeping, rolling on the floor and pulling her hair like a lunatic person. Sadij was so bewildered by his mother's peculiar and dramatic behaviour that he assumed that she had gone mad.

To lessen his mother's hysteria, he started to speak calmly, and tried to reason with her, '*Listen, Ma, it's no use spluttering and frothing, you're only hurting yourself. Don't ever accept to be a punching bag. If there are marks and bruises, get photos, support your case with those photos and get the police*

146

involved, or seek help from self-help groups set up for violence against women. *Whatever you do, just don't keep quiet. He has no right to beat you up. He's a terrible person and there's absolutely nothing you will ever do that can change that. Once you leave him, he will fight his demons alone.'*

Makiera spoke again in a highly pitched voice, '*How I wish I could work on my marriage and get it to a healthy enough state, then that would be better for your brothers.'*

Sadij had a hunch that his mother had no intention of breaking up with Ablah, and attempted to convince her to quit her bullying husband. '*Come on, Ma, your relationship is no longer working. You're miserable. Love is gone. It's time to split up. Otherwise, you will end up cold and dead in a ditch. Is that what you want? I know by now you're so broken and made to feel so insecure that you feel like you love this coward too much to leave. I know it's scary and a bit hard for you. You're wondering what will happen to you and my brothers, and how you will live, but when you make the right decision, everything will fall into place. But you're a better judge of that than I am.'*

He had no sooner finished speaking when a nurse came in to administer a tranquiliser to Mrs Makiera, and at the same time, she informed Sadij that visiting hours were over. Therefore, Sadij took leave of his mother and left.

Chapter 8

Notwithstanding, Sabira and Sadij's advice, Makiera had resigned herself to the idea that staying in a loveless relationship for her children was an undertaking that was worth attempting. She felt it in her bones that staying for her children was in their best interest in terms of security and stability; moreover, she felt guilty about having caused so much pain and anguish to her son, Sadij, in the wake of her divorce from her former husband. Therefore, she couldn't afford to make the same mistake again. She strongly believed that if she and Ablah pitched in and could work on their failing relationship to get their union back on track, that would be better for the kids. As far as Makiera was concerned, she pretended to her children that she and her husband were just doing fine; but as the days wore on, she realised that she was merely fooling herself, and wasn't being honest with her children. She had compromised more than seventeen years of her happiness to stay together and spare her children the trouble of developing social, behavioural, emotional and academic problems. She wanted to wait until her third little boy finished high school to call it quits. She had an issue that kept bothering her and wasn't sure whether she could put up with it any longer. Ablah's claim that he couldn't control his anger was nonsense, for she noticed that he had always managed to curb his aggressive emotions when he was with other people. So, why not with someone he used to call 'my soul mate'? The situation got more and more intolerable; she hadn't left any stone unturned, she had exhausted all options to save her marriage, but to no avail. Ablah's petulance and aggressive behaviour was a cycle that he was not willing to break. The physical and emotional pain that he daily inflicted upon Makiera was huge and interminable. To Makiera, living with someone she was perpetually afraid of was daunting.

Finally, she decided to take daring steps to leave her man. They finally split up and Ablah was forced to move out. Managing on his own was not easy, for he got used to taking Makiera for a ride. Thereby, he decided to beg her to come back after few weeks of separation.

Chapter 9

It was a very cold evening. The wind was blowing so violently that it rattled the open window in the kitchen, sending the plastic plates put in the draining rack reeling down the corridor. Then a heavy rain came tumbling down and the roof was leaking; after a few minutes, Makiera suddenly noticed water dripping from the ceiling. She tried not to panic, reassuring her youngest child that it was a minor inconvenience and that he didn't need to worry. Her first main concern was to prevent the water that started to flow abundantly from damaging her furniture and other electrical appliances.

While she was doing her best to minimise the damages, the bell rang. She didn't have time to answer the door, for she went in the kitchen, grabbed a bucket and placed it under the leak to capture any water leaking into the house. She then took a long towel to dry up the wet areas. This time, the visitor – seeing that no one came to open the door – kept rapping at the door.

Makiera, in a very feeble voice, asked, *'Who is it?'*

The stranger replied in an entreating tone, *'It's me Ablah. Will you please open the door?'*

Makiera tried to pull herself together to appear stronger and in control, and asked, *'What on earth do you want?'*

Ablah made another earnest appeal, *'May I have a word with you?'*

Makiera determined not to let him in rebuffed his request. *'There's nothing left to be said. Go or else I'll call the police.'*

It seemed that her former husband had no intention of capitulating; then he changed his strategy and decided to tug at her heartstrings, evoking the happy moments they had spent together and showing great concern for the future of his children. *'For heaven's sake, open that damned door. It won't be too long. I just need to talk to you.'*

Seeing that Ablah was adamant that he wasn't going anywhere until she opened the door, she opened it, and in came Ablah, staggering drunk on his thin legs, advancing into the middle of the house. As there were some small pools of water on the floor, he lost a secure footing and skidded on the puddle.

When he got up, he asked, *'Makiera, tell me it's not true. Are you cleaning the floor at this time of day?'*

Makiera was extremely upset by the leak in her roof and was in no mood for chewing the fat. *'Can't you see I'm on tenterhooks all evening trying to fix that damned leak in the roof?'*

Sadij was so hammered that he started slurring and mumbling words that Makiera found hard to understand; she then ordered him to leave, as it was getting too late. He then flung himself down on the sofa, tilted his head and held a pillow close by to attenuate the brightness of the lightbulb that made him squint and said in a very funny manner, *'Listen, honey, don't lose sleep over it. I'll fix it for you.'*

He got up, but since he had no control over his body, he fidgeted and stumbled. His eyes were glossy and drifted around the living room; he smiled more broadly than he would if he were sober. Makiera didn't know how to get rid of his cumbersome presence, always thinking about the leak in the roof. He got up again, took hold of a chair nearby to keep from falling over and walked toward the bucket in which the leaking water was falling. His footsteps were irregular, and his body was going to lurch as he tried hard to keep his balance.

Then, he said, '*Just allow me to find out where the leak is coming from, darling.*'

Makiera knew that Ablah was tipsy and didn't know what he was saying. She then told him, '*Listen, Ablah. This is a very tough task, and you just can't cut it. Besides, it's none of your business. Please leave me alone. I just want to be on my own.*'

He started to reminisce about the joyful moments they had been together, apologised to her for his past mistakes, promised to never make the same mistakes again, and repeated the same refrain, '*I love you and I can't live without you. I want you back in my life.*'

He got teary-eyed and physically clingy to Makiera, expressing remorse for having done things that Makiera herself didn't know he was responsible for. He confessed to having been a silly and uncaring husband and promised that he would atone for the bad things he had done in the past.

Finally, Makiera, who was still bearing a grudge against him, said with tears in her eyes, '*How can I possibly take you back after all the anguish you've put my whole life through? I will never feel safe and happy with you again. Listen, Ablah. This is neither the time nor the place to discuss this. Plus, it's almost midnight, and I have to turn in, 'cause I've got to wake up early for work tomorrow and drop off your kids at school. So, I'm begging you to leave now. We will discuss this in more detail tomorrow.*'

She walked up to the front door of the house, opened it and implored him to go at once. Though he was under the influence of alcohol and virtually legless, he, tucking his shirt in halfway, slowly left, wobbling along the street.

Chapter 10

Makiera was really in a quandary as to whether or not to take Ablah back and start over; reconciling with her ex-husband turned out to be a complicated issue that was fraught with mixed emotions. To make the right call, Makiera decided to seek her intimate friend's advice. To that end, she paid a short visit to Sabira, who knew both Makiera and Ablah quite well.

Therefore, Makiera believed that any tip or observation coming from a person that had known both of them and was witness to their relationship would undoubtedly be very helpful. Makiera started by giving her friend a very succinct account of what came to pass yesterday, and how earnest Ablah seemed to be when he said he wanted her back in his life.

Sabira narrowed her eyes, looking doubtfully at her friend, and said, '*I see.*' But her eyes betrayed that she didn't really believe it.

To elicit Makiera's take on the idea of reconciling with her ex-husband, she asked, '*Listen, my friend. Matters of the heart are intensely personal. I appreciate your seeking my advice on the matter, but I think that you need to listen to your heart first. Tell me how do you feel about this reconciliation? Are you tempted to get back together, knowing that he's been beating you up and very abusive? Do you think he's changed since the relationship ended?*'

Sabira was waiting for a resolute reply from Makiera; but the latter seemed to be confused, worried and at a loss. After hesitating for a few minutes, she blurted it out, *'If I told you something, do you promise not to be mad at me?'*

Sabira, in a reassuring voice, said, *'How could I fall out with the best and most honest friend I've ever had in my life?'*

She, at last, opened her heart to Sabira. *'I desperately want him back too. I just want with all my heart to have our relationship back despite all the pain he has caused me. You just can't imagine to what length I'm ready to go to make our union stronger than before. And now that he came yesterday, telling me he wanted me to be back in his life and that he can't live without me... I think everyone deserves a second chance. I believe that that short-lived period of separation has taught him a lot. He has realised that he can't adjust to living away from me and the children.'*

Sabira started casting dubious looks at her friend, for she couldn't believe what she heard. She was taking all that was said with a pinch of salt, hoping that all of this was just a dream. Seeing that her friend was taken in by Ablah's bogus apology, she tried her utmost to bring Makiera to reason.

She then asked her a very embarrassing question, *'Has it ever occurred to you to ask yourself why he wants you back?'*

This disconcerting question set Makiera blushing, breathing heavily and breaking into a sweat. A few seconds later, she endeavoured to gather her wits and get through this slippery question.

'Of course, he must be missing me.'

That was the last straw that broke the camel's back. Sabira lost her patience and said what she thought about the whole thing, without regard to how Makiera would take it.

'*To be honest with you, the only thing he's missing is your financial help, the good things you always do to make life easier for him, the special presents you usually offer him, the great care you take of his parents whenever they come to visit. At no time in his entire life has that selfish scrounger cared about you and your kids! That's the real truth that you've always been running away from. And if you think that staying in a loveless relationship for the kids is worth trying, then take the plunge; after all, this is your life.*'

She was waiting for Makiera's reaction, but no response ensued. Makiera was struck dumb with astonishment and surprise, for she didn't expect Sabira to spit it out. The latter paused, waiting for a reaction from Makiera, but nothing happened, then she proceeded, '*You only have one life, do you want to spend it miserable?*'

It took Makiera a while to find her voice; at last, she resignedly said, '*I just don't want to break up my family. And I think I owe my relationship a chance to improve.*'

To which Sabira responded, '*Well, if you think that this is the right decision, then I wish you good luck.*'

As soon as Sabira's husband got back home, the two ladies switched gears. A few minutes later, Makiera left.

Chapter 11

Makiera had finally decided to rekindle the romance with Ablah because she seemed to think that the grass wasn't greener on the divorced side. Besides, she firmly believed that staying together for her children and keeping the family united was the best thing to do. Rather than taking heed of Sabira's advice, Makiera had decided to focus on her intuition and gut feelings.

Eventually, her inner wisdom tipped the balance in favour of reconciliation. Now that they got together again, Makiera worked harder at saving her marriage, always thinking that keeping the nuclear family intact was the right thing to do. To her, the children's stability and security came first. She also believed that with time, she might be able to get her relationship with Ablah to a healthy state. To build a strong foundation for her conjugal life, Makiera was convinced that setting new conditions was the first step that she needed to take; she for the first time had acted boldly, defending her rights and setting the tone for her future relationship with Ablah. She told him what she wanted her marriage to look like.

She cleared her throat and began listing her conditions. *'First, no more battering, and no more emotional abuse. Is this clear?'*

Ablah agreed with great alacrity. During the first weeks,

Ablah gave Makiera the impression that he had changed for the better; but as time went by, the mask that he was wearing finally fell off. All of a sudden, that ostensibly heavenly bliss turned into a real hell; all that specious promise of being loving, caring, respectful turned out to be a humbug. He was only loving in public, but as soon as they were both behind closed doors, he started biting her head off over petty things, yelling at her so loudly that she became scared in her own home, almost urging her to leave her abode in quest of peace.

He became so mean to her that one day she grabbed the phone and called Sabira. '*You're right, my friend. What's bred in the bone will come out in the flesh. It is the same crap again. I can't take it any more.*'

She spoke in a brittle voice, sounding as if she were about to cry. '*I just can't tell you how I feel. He has become more sarcastic and belittling than before, and he's doing this in front of the children. Most of the time, I try to turn a deaf ear to his demeaning comments and put-downs; I'm afraid, but sometimes I get the impression that I'm letting myself get used to his mocking and disparaging remarks.*' Her voice got wobbly because she was crying. '*All the put-downs he always makes have ended up wearing my self-confidence away; he's treating me as if I'm not equal.*'

All that Makiera was looking for was emotional support from her intimate friend. Sabira knew that the only thing Makiera wanted was to be listened to; that was why she kept quiet and listened with rapt attention to her friend. Sabira did hit the nail right on the head with her silence. There were so many things that Makiera wanted to share with Sabira that she asked her if they could get together and talk.

'*I hope you don't mind, dearest one, but is it possible for you to take time out of your busy schedule so that we can discuss this at leisure?'*

Sabira agreed at once and the two ladies met up in a café that wasn't far from where Sabira was taking up residence. They chose to sit at a table that was located in an isolated corner of the café so that no one would be able to eavesdrop on their conversation.

Mrs Sabira tilted her head to the side and watched Makiera speaking her piece.

'You can't imagine how painful it is to feel that your husband doesn't care about your feelings, and this only means that he wants to leave me.'

Sabira reacted, saying, *'Well, if both of you agree that you're no longer making each other happy, at least you're giving each other the chance to savour happiness outside of your married life.'*

Makiera, taken aback by what her friend had just said, asked, *'I just can't see what you mean. Are you suggesting I need to look for happiness elsewhere?'*

Sabira replied, *'The point is Ablah is continually hurting your feelings and that is not okay. As I told you last time, he's a selfish bully. Perhaps he's always been selfish, and you didn't know his true colours because you were enthralled with him. The problem now is that his unacceptable behaviour is upsetting you and causing you much anguish. Besides, you've broached this with him several times, and up to now, he hasn't stopped acting in such a selfish manner. How many times have you told me that he doesn't value your time nor all the things you do to make things easier for him? Do I have to remind you? And one more thing that exasperates me is that you're financially being put upon by that filthy scrounger. Do you want me to go on enumerating all his defects? Come on, Makiera, enough is enough. You have to terminate this loveless relationship. Otherwise, he's going to ditch you. Look at yourself! You're getting older and you're losing value as you age. So, in an unhealthy and unsafe relationship like yours, divorce is the best course of action to take. My position has always been clear, and this is what I have told you several times. But you just don't seem to listen.'*

Makiera was just listening, leaning upon her folded arms, her brows drawn together, her gaze clouding and going distant; she seemed to be confused and at a loss. She opened and closed her mouth several times before uttering a single word.

She took a deep breath and finally let it out, *'When I first got married, I thought that marriage is all about to give and take. I have always felt good being on the side that gives without counting; I must admit that I have always gone into raptures every time I discover that generous part of me. But you know, sometimes, you know one grows tired of being put upon and on the side that gives. And I have always said to myself, well, maybe one day Ablah may end up being on the side that gives. I kept deluding myself with the notion that as long as we're living together, it doesn't matter who gives and who takes. I have waited and anticipated, hoping that one day he's going to change. But it finally dawned upon me that Ablah has always been taking me for granted and that what has mattered to him all that long is my money and my flat, and nothing else. How silly of me not to have noticed this a long time ago!'*

Sabira painted a ray of sunshine over her face; her eyes sparkled because she, at last, could see her friend freeing herself from deception. She hugged her intimate friend and

159

said, '*Oh, dear, I'm proud of you. A person can never thrive in a relationship wherein there's no reciprocity. Now, you have to take a final and peremptory decision. I mean you need to engage an attorney because guys like Ablah are likely to refuse to pay child support, especially you got two kids that haven't reached age eighteen yet. And since you're gonna be the custodial parent, Ablah is supposed to pay you the alimony. But this time, promise me that you won't let him hoodwink you by his spurious apologies. Because if you do, you have to forget that you have a friend named Sabira. Do you hear me?*'

Makiera immediately responded, '*I swear, this will never happen again.*'

Two days later, Makiera hired the services of a renowned lawyer who set the process of ending her union with Ablah into motion. And since there were no assets to be divided between the two partners, Ablah was ordered to leave Makiera's flat and make child support payments.

Chapter 12

After ending her twenty-two-year marriage with Ablah, Makiera realised that involving her minor children in the childish game of he said / she said, as she had done with Taib, was a stupid idea, for it had been nearly twenty-five years since Taib hadn't heard from his only son. Sadij had all along been mad at his father and blamed Taib entirely for having divorced his mother. That was why she decided to keep her version of the story to herself. Makiera, a controlling and toxic mother, had never realised the excruciating pain and anguish she had inflicted upon Taib, encouraging Sadij to block his father from all communication. How many letters had been left unanswered? How many emails had remained unanswered? Makiera's rancour had pushed her to refuse to inform her son of Taib's phone calls, thinking that in doing so, she was taking her revenge on Sadij's father. Her selfishness had induced her to prevent Taib from providing his only son with the emotional support he was desperately in need of.

Now, she began to have some pangs of consciousness and guilt, for all the intimate acquaintances that Sadij had attempted to strike turned sour and failed. Now, she realised that Taib was a scarce pearl that she had foolishly let slip through her fingers, and that was why she was thinking about how to fix that father-son relationship. After a long and deep reflection, she decided to talk to her son about his father and tell him how loving and good he was. Sadij's decision to cut his father out of his life was instigated by his toxic mother, Makiera, who, at an early age, kept instilling into her son's mind that his father had never taken the trouble to contact him. She had finally managed to bury her ex-husband alive, severing any potential bond between father and son.

Although Sadij tried to hide the inward grief he felt deep inside – grief that was all the more poignant and confusing as it related to the loss of a person who hadn't died, who had merely vanished from his son's life, but was living somewhere else, that family estrangement had made Sadij insecure in his relationships. Makiera had reached a point where she became aware that things could have been different had she not been selfish and grudging. Were it not for the pain that Ablah had made her endure, she would never have thought about patching things up between Sadij and his father? But a greater part of Sadij kept telling him that there was no point in getting together with his father, as he was no longer in need of him. Every time Makiera tried to broach the subject with her son, the latter kept repeating that he wasn't ready yet for that, and asked her to give him some time to get his thoughts in order.

Today, Makiera was expecting her son to come and have lunch together. She knew that her son was fond of Moroccan couscous with seven vegetables. Everything was in place; the table was set and ready; and there came a soft knock on the door. Makiera walked up to the front door, opened it and to her amazement, in came her son Sadij, who was holding a bunch of flowers in his hand.

As soon as she caught sight of lavish cream and lavender roses mix, her face brightened up; she then took that wonderland long-stem purple roses bouquet, arranged it in a coloured glass vase, and said, '*You know I love flowers; they just help me feel secure and relaxed. Your dad used to tell me to keep flowers around the home because they greatly reduce the stress level. Oh, thank you so much, dearest one. You're an angel.*'

Sadij's eyebrows were raised and arched to express surprise. He was wondering why his mother recalled his father telling her to have flowers around. So, Sadij's jaw dropped and his eyes were wide open. Seeing that her son was a bit puzzled by her alluding to his father in the conversation, she braced herself for his imminently corrosive comments. But nothing happened.

She then explained that Taib was in a league of his own in that he was a very diligent man, who had never taken advantage of anyone. '*At no time has your dad used me in a wrong way. He always gives and takes less, unlike that selfish and unethical exploiter.*'

She did even refrain from mentioning the name of her second husband. She paused and released a deep sigh of regret and despondency. Sajid was extremely shocked by this unexpected avowal of his mother, creating a seismic shift in her take on his father. He just couldn't believe what she was saying, and abruptly questioned his mother's insanity.

'*Have you gone stark raving mad? Get your head out of the sand. That ain't the way you used to talk about him. You're just making this up. Aren't you? You've got to be kidding me, Mother!*'

Makiera found herself in a real scrape, for she didn't know how to go about it; this time, she was more determined than ever before to tell the truth, come what may.

'*That's not the point I'm trying to make. Just open your*

ears. Your dad, unlike that scum of the earth, is no freeloader.'
Sadij asked for an explanation. *'I don't follow you. What do you mean?'*

Makiera, attempting to put an end to this misunderstanding, said, *'Let me make myself clear. Your dad is an honest man; he has never used others for personal gain. Whereas, Ablah is a sponger.'*

Showing disbelief, Sadij said, *'Please, Mum. Don't pull the wool over my eyes. The guy you're taking up the cudgels for, right now, is the man that walked out on us a long time ago. So, why are you saying he's a nice and honest person now? Can't you just remember how lonely I felt, with no one to turn to for help? I will never forget how deeply I sank into a state of sadness and anxiety. Sometimes, I get the terrible sensation that I will never get over it. For heaven's sake, don't ever mention his name in my presence, and keep your ideas to yourself. Besides, why have you waited until now to tell me this? It's too late. I don't need him any longer. Things could have been different if you had told me this a long time ago. Instead, you've always put your own needs first. It has never occurred to you to care about my feelings. You've always shown favouritism towards my half-brothers.'*

After that encounter with his mother, Sadij felt dejected and downhearted; the painful memories of calling him names, pointing out his defects and deliberately raising things he was very sensitive about resurfaced, and caused his body to tense up and his stomach to churn. Convinced that his manipulative and toxic mother was about to turn the tables on him through her twisting the truth to make herself look good, getting emotionally reactive, and blaming it all on others, he decided to boogie.

Chapter 13

Makiera had been extremely lonely and depressed since Ablah moved out last September. Her solitariness got more intense since that last encounter with her son. Worse than that, her being by herself led her to intemperate consumption of alcohol and binge eating. After her split, she felt also rejected by her married friends, who no longer wanted to hang out with her. She knew that this was certainly an ineluctable fallout from her divorce, which added more anguish to an already distressing situation. She had been a single mother for two years now. And only now was it dawning upon her the monstrousness of what being on one's own entailed; there was no one that could save her from slipping into that dismal abyss of isolation.

She had four children: Ashraf, Talal, and Yasser with Ablah, and Sadij with Taib. Ablah lived miles away from his children and had very little involvement in their lives. Makiera was divorced and didn't have to sort out finances because there wasn't that much that could be shared between Makiera and Ablah, except for a house they bought a long time ago in Morocco.

On this issue, Makiera decided to make a fair agreement with Ablah, without having to go to court, because she was worried about how much that would cost her if she ever hired the services of a lawyer; that was why she accepted to negotiate directly with Ablah. They sold the house they had bought on the seaside of Saidia, in the city of Oujda, and went shares. She outwardly pretended to be happy, but then she kept saying to herself that things could have been worse, come to think of it. When in the company of her relatives and members of her family, she held back her tears till she could unobtrusively cry without being noticed by anyone. She felt fortunate every time her elder son, Sadij, got back to her. But whenever the poor young man introduced his girlfriend to his mama, the latter just hated her for no obvious reason. She morbidly believed that no girl hitherto introduced was good enough for her son. She mistakenly thought that no girl knew her son better than she did, and the notion of a girl stepping in and stealing her son's heart wasn't welcome.

Bringing a girlfriend home was a taboo in Sadij's father's time; but in Sadij's permissive and open-minded society, dating a girl or a boy was commonplace. This time, Sadij brought his beloved girlfriend, Sarah. That was the first time Sarah was going to meet Makiera. Her hair was ebony-black and it tumbled over her shoulders. Her sugar-sweet lips couldn't go unnoticed. She had an elegant character. She was wearing a voguish skirt in an offbeat manner. When she spoke, a set of sparkling white teeth gently gleamed; her fascinating and innocent brown eyes gazed at Makiera, as Sadij tried to introduce them to each other.

'Ma, I'd like you to meet my friend, Sarah.'

Instead of welcoming her warmly into her family, Makiera kept looking at her from head to toe. Sarah wanted to hug Sadij's mother, but the latter extended her arm for a handshake and took the wrapped gift Sarah had brought. Shortly after their arrival, Sadij's mum asked him to mow the lawn of a very small garden attached to her ground floor flat, since, according to her, he did a more careful job than a gardener. She asked him to do it so she and Sarah would be left alone. To find out whether Sarah had any of her son's best interests at heart, Makiera kicked into high gear and started molesting Sadij's girlfriend with embarrassing questions. Makiera wasn't interested in being around and talking to Sarah, and that was why she was distancing herself from her son's girlfriend. As Makiera started speaking, she kept her arms closed in front of Sarah.

'What do you do?'

'I work as a substitute teacher in the American School of Paris,' the young lady answered, with a slight tremor in her voice.

Makiera, unable to make out what was meant by that, kept insisting. *'What does your job consist of?'* Makiera was looking away from Sarah while asking.

Sarah knew that Makiera's shifting her eyes to other things around her was a tell-tale sign that she didn't like her. She thereby decided not to pick up on any negativity from Sadij's mother, and responded politely, *'A substitute teacher is a teacher who replaces teachers who are absent from work.'*

Makiera rolled her eyes at that and said, *'What? You're just like a spare tire.'* Makiera was judging Sarah's job in a way that showed she was looking down upon her. She didn't even give her the floor to talk and explain.

Sarah was about to inform her that the teaching position she was having was just provisional when Makiera, dominating the conversation, rudely kept cutting her off. Sarah was overwhelmed by a peculiar feeling of wanting to run and hide that seemed to run through her whole body. She began to blush.

To offend Sarah more and more, she asked her, '*Has Sadij ever talked to you about his little cousin Jalila? I don't think he did. Well, she's an engineer. She's got a very good salary and has a flat that's hers.*'

Sarah immediately realised that Makiera was a shallow lady and everything about her was forced. She kept sending phony smiles at Sarah. Makiera wasn't ready to give Sarah a break yet.

She then asked her, '*Tell me, Miss, are you a good cook?*'

Sarah felt as if she were being interrogated by the police at a police station. She tried not to overreact and did her best to make a good impression on Makiera. She even managed to show her that she wasn't upset or sad. She eventually reassured Sadij's mother that she was very fond of cooking and spent time surfing the net in an attempt to spot some trendy dishes. The only thing that Sarah wanted was to have some peace and to make a success of her relationship with Sadij, and that was why she tried to adjust and behave naively for the initial period of her relationship with Sadij's mother. The latter looked through the French door that opened directly onto the garden, waved her hand at her son and went on talking.

'*Do you know what Sadij's favourite dish is?*'

Sarah started feeling like a worthless mess, but tried not to let her limited knowledge in cooking take a toll on her relationship with Sadij; she then replied, '*Honestly, I don't, but I would be more than happy if you could just tell me what his favourite dish is.*'

Makiera paused for a while, her feet and her torso pointing away from Sarah, and in a standoffish manner said, '*I guess you just don't know my son. And you're trying to find recipes in cookbooks, online or magazines is simply a waste of time. A mother must teach her daughter the basics of cooking techniques, seasoning and all that stuff.'*

No sooner had she finished saying hurtful and mean things to Sarah than Sadij made an appearance just in time to spare Sarah more torturing. As soon as Makiera caught a glimpse of her son standing on the doorstep, she became so nice that Sadij would have trouble believing Sarah if the latter ever complained about his mother smothering her with rude and snide remarks when he wasn't around. Sarah knew that the ultimate test of the future of her relationship with Sadij largely depended upon meeting Sadij's mother and getting her approval and blessing. But deep down, she was afraid that Sadij's mother might want to always have the upper hand.

While Sarah was pondering about the outcome of her relationship with Sadij, the latter joined his mother, who was in the kitchen, to prepare Moroccan tea, for he was adept in the matter. He took a teapot from the cupboard, put the tea in it, poured in some boiling water, swirled gently to warm pot and rinse tea, strained out and discarded water, reserving tea leaves in the pot. While filling the teapot with boiled water to the brim, he asked his mother, *'What do you think of Sarah, Mum?'*

After a moment's hesitation, she at last said, *'Well, she seems to be a sweet girl, but I don't think you both have what it takes to make both people happy.'*

Sadij was taken aback by his mother's opinion on Sarah; he knew that his girlfriend was spontaneous, home-trained and free from artificiality and affectation. He, therefore, asked his mother an embarrassing question, *'How do you know that Sarah isn't good for me?'*

As Sadij was stirring in sugar to taste, Makiera grabbed her son by the scruff of his neck and said, *'Listen, my son! Only a woman can truly know and see through another woman. Remember this, this woman will never make you happy. She comes from a very poor family. Besides, she's having a provisional job. How will both of you make both ends meet? What if you have kids?'*

Sadij, beside himself with anger, said, *'Mum, you're a piece of work. You're unable to get along with any girl I bring home, and you're too judgmental. I'm a full-fledged adult, and I do know what's right for me.'*

Makiera's anger was beyond measure, for she had always believed she could never be wrong. She dropped the plate that was full of traditional Moroccan pastries onto the floor, and yelled at her son, *'If you know that girl quite well, why are you asking my opinion? You both go to hell, and don't ever bring any girl in this house.'*

Sadij found himself and his girlfriend chased out of the house. He was really ashamed and didn't know what to say to Sarah. Being critical about everything her son did was one thing, but expelling him and humiliating him in front of his girlfriend was more than anyone could take.

Chapter 14

Though Ablah moved out a long time ago, Makiera couldn't forgive the anguish he had caused her. She hadn't had another relationship since she separated from him, and even if she wanted to have another man in her life, this just didn't happen; she felt so depressed at the idea of spending the rest of her life on her own, especially when her younger son, Yasser, came of age and decided to enlist in the French army. That feeling of loneliness got more poignant, especially when not one of her children came to visit her. Her network of social relationships was deficient in both quality and quantity.

As a consequence, she couldn't help feeling like nobody wanted her. She knew that presenting herself as a sad and very miserable woman wasn't going to be attractive to people around her. To get out of this wretched situation, she decided to change the way she looked; to that end, she dyed her hair, wore revealing clothes and a lot of make-up. Then, she got enrolled in a lonely-hearts club on the Internet. All the guys she had met on the dating website were merely looking for a flirtation with no consequences. Her search for a soul mate turned out to be on a wild goose chase. She then tried to take a holiday with a man she had made acquaintance with on the net; they both travelled to Marrakech on a package tour.

Unfortunately, Makiera realised that she was just a meaningless fling to that French man. Before her return to

France, an eccentric idea crossed her mind. She said to herself, *'Why not get in touch with Taib. Nothing ventured, nothing gained.'* Whereupon, she called Taib, and arranged a time and place to meet. The two hadn't seen each other for almost twenty-nine years and their reunion was a joyous occasion.

When Taib saw her, he found out that she had changed almost beyond recognition. Loss of muscle tone and thinning skin had given her face a drooping appearance. Her face had no longer that plump and smooth surface that she used to be proud of; her thin face showing the wearing effects of worry and suffering was covered with little wrinkles that she tried hard to cover up with concealer. However, her getting addicted to cigarette smoking and gin had made them develop more quickly. As soon as she caught sight of Taib, she waved at him. He walked up to her, kissed her and sat next to her.

She launched the conversation. *'How are you doing? And how are you getting on with your work?'*

Taib was struck by her sudden and unexpected interest in how and what he was doing, remained dumbfounded for a moment and then replied, *'Long time, no see! What are you doing in this neck of the woods? Honestly, I've never thought I'd see you here. As far as I'm concerned, I have nothing to complain about. Thank, God. How about you? How's Sadij doing? I tried to contact you several times, but you just kept hanging up on me and telling me to never call you again. You've told me that your husband is very jealous, and then you entreated me to leave you alone. Whereas the only thing I wanted was to ask after my son, and I think at least I'm entitled to that.'*

Sensing that Taib was about to fume because of her wicked attempts at estranging him from his son, she immediately struck a very sensitive chord in Taib.

'I have been under the weather. I have recently undergone liver resection because I was suffering from liver cancer. Besides, I'm currently going through a somewhat difficult fix at the family and relationship level. In 1998, Ablah and I celebrated our union religiously, with witnesses, without making it official at the town hall. He was already engaged in a divorce procedure and had no children from his first union. At the end of our first year of marriage, Ashraf was born, then Talal a year later, in 2000. The difficulties and problems in our relationship began very quickly right afterward, for many reasons that I will discuss preferably another time, because it is very complicated, and I don't have time, as I have a plane to catch in less than two hours.'

Taib immediately felt empathy for her and told her that she could always rely on him. Before they said goodbye to each other, they exchanged their email addresses to remain in touch.

Chapter 15

In the process of her divorce from Ablah, Makiera, as customary, had played the role of the victim to her advantage; she was so selfish with the fruit of her womb that she would act helpless and desperate in such a way that made Talal, Ashraf and Yasser feel sorry for her; she had also told lies about her first husband Taib to her now estranged son, Sadij, to gain preference. Her playing the victim was in both cases fuelled by ire, indignation and vengeance. All her other children from Ablah were only subjected to her emotionally abusive behaviour for a short time, for in no time, it dawned upon them that their manipulative mother's behaviour was carefully calculated to take revenge on their father. All her children knew without the slightest shadow of a doubt that Makiera was not a person to be trusted. Feeling abandoned by everyone, she turned to Taib. She wrote him a letter.

Dear Taib,
I hope you're doing pretty well. I arrived home safely yesterday. Your words and sympathy were too strong and made me feel happy and sad at the same time; I find it difficult to express my emotions. Either way, I think it's a good thing that we put an end to a silence that has gone on for too long. We have a son together and our very special story cannot be suspended in time until our death. Our son, Sadij, has roots

and origins that he must get to know better for himself and his descendants, God willing. Peace, serenity and good health are the best we can wish for him, but also both of us. Therefore, I promise to do everything I can to work out our differences. From now on, wisdom must be our engine of life. I am very happy that we had this opportunity to see each other again. We have aged (a little...) but I found the Taib whom I knew with a heart full of kindness and a pure soul. I wish you all the best. Be careful not to idealise me too much over time. I think that you are sincere, I also feel very close to you and I have the impression of reading you like a book, despite the long-distance and time that has separated us.

Looking forward to hearing from you real soon.
Makiera

As soon as Taib had read Makiera's message, he set about answering her message.

Dear Makiera,
I'm so glad you arrived safely. The feelings I expressed when we met at Marrakech airport emanate from a sincere heart. I just don't know how to thank you for thinking about contacting me, and above all for wanting to help me get back with our son, after a long and painful breakup – a breakup that has hurt the three of us too much. I hope this message won't be the last. My presence and unconditional love are what my son, Sadij, really needs; I'll do whatever it may take to make up for the lost time.

Looking forward to reading from you.
Taib

In the meantime, Sadij was unable to create real and lasting love with all the girls he encountered. On the level of his imagination, he knew that love was the most wonderful and greatest thing that could happen to a person in life. But up to now, he had never managed to have a loving relationship that could stand the test of time. When going out with nymphs offline didn't work, Sadij decided to try online dating. To find the right person, he downloaded several dating applications. He erased and remade his profile several times. This idea of trying love-finding applications was Jaaba's suggestion. He told Sadij that the Internet had helped some friends of his to find romantic relationships and soul mates.

However, Sadij discovered that online matching wasn't much of a success as a reliable tool to discover a potential person with whom he could have a strong affinity. He made a very striking discovery. He realised that all the girls he met online tried to make themselves appear as enthralling as possible to woo his heart and mind; he concluded that building a relationship on lies and flimsy foundations would crumble sooner or later. Sadij was shocked more than once when he went out with some Parisian blondes whose main concern was income and wealth more than anything else.

On one occasion, he came across an odd nymph who preferred to go out with a tall guy that had a strong and sturdy physique. Neither that type of artificial, online contact nor the direct interpersonal interactions did come up to Sadij's expectations. Sadij's lack of self-confidence did wreak havoc on all personal relationships that he had vainly attempted to sustain. To get rid of his insecurities, he decided to travel around Europe; he made a trip to Macedonia, a country in south-eastern Europe. He landed in Skopje, the capital and largest city of North Macedonia. The first thing that caught Sadij's eye when he set foot in this quirky place was that there were more statues than people around. That was the first time he had ever visited this place. So, he had no idea about how this place looked like. He was very lucky, for at this time of the year the weather was warm and sunny. He stayed there for two days and had time to see all sights; he above all enjoyed the coffee. So, he went into a coffee shop (The House) where he ordered some home-made coffee, along with a copious healthy breakfast made from oats and fruit. The waiter was nice and friendly. He spoke French and English, and Sadij felt very comfortable in that he could finally elicit information about the place from that guy.

'I just would like to know if there's any natural scenery close by. I mean, I'm very fond of hiking. You know I need to leave all the hustle and bustle of Paris behind.'

'I see. I recommend you to go on a hike from the village of Janche and discover the village of Galichnick. I'm sure you will enjoy the spectacular view during your walk.'

'Oh, c'est bien gentil de votre part. Merci infiniment, monsieur.'

'De rien. Je vous souhaite une excellente randonnée.'

Sadij sipped his espresso, tipped the waiter and left. He then went on a pleasant hike through splendid mountain landscapes, walking along a path that united the village of Janche to the village of Galichnik. It was a really fine day; the sun was shining. He stopped by at a farmer's barn where some people were offered some local cheese to taste; he walked up to the crowd, greeted them and had his share of the tasty cheese. He took a piece of local yellow cheese called Kashkaval, bit it and found that it had a piquant, spicy and somewhat salty taste with a slight hint of olive oil; it had the same taste as the cheddar cheese in Somerset. Since he found it palatable, he bought some and returned to Skopje, where he stayed in Ibis Styles Skopje. That modest and cheap hotel was very close to the city centre. He took a shower, took his mobile, got connected, checked his Facebook page and found a message sent by Taib, read it but didn't reply as usual. Just as he was trying hard to keep anxiety and feelings of insecurity at bay, the trauma of his absent father came galloping in long and quick strides to pester him. He couldn't banish the idea of growing up with a father who was emotionally and physically absent from his mind, because he was reluctant to acknowledge its existence. All the hatred that he felt towards Taib was mainly triggered by the negative and devastating comments that Makiera used to make when he was just five years old, and which stuck with him today. The increased levels of fear and insecurity plagued him, and did impinge upon everything in his life, and more importantly his intimate personal relationships.

Whenever he made acquaintance with a girl, he found it hard to sustain his relationship with her and ended up parting with her. Right after his return from Skopje, he resumed his work at Sanofi. One fine afternoon, while having a break, he met Sandrine, a fellow worker. She was newly hired by the company; they were both working in the same department. He got along with her, from the first drink and quick chat they had together, Sadij felt she was congenial to him. Sadij wasn't on the prowl for a passionate hook-up or a flirty crush at all. He was desperately in need of a girl to be with, probably for good.

Sandrine was a self-assured young woman, five years older than him. She was good-looking, slim, with some freckles on her cheek that made her so cute. She had long blonde hair that she liked to wear curly. Whenever there was any decision to make, he would seek Sandrine's opinion.

At one point, he wanted to paint his bedroom in a new apartment he rented in the fifteenth district, and didn't know what colour to use. He then asked Sandrine, *'I would be obliged if you could just tell me which colour to use to paint my sleeping room.'*

Sandrine was surprised, and some horizontal wrinkles were drawn across her forehead. She said, with upper lip raised and the lower one drawn down, *'I just don't know. I mean you're the one that's going to sleep in it. I'm afraid I can't be of any help to you. Tastes differ.'*

He kept insisting, *'I don't care. Just tell me which colour you would use to paint your bedroom?'*

Sensing that Sadij wouldn't bugger off until she gave him an answer, she therefore replied, *'Well, if I were you, I would paint it purple.'*

He thanked her, saying, *'I'll paint it pink, for sure.'*

Sandrine didn't appreciate having someone who was so heavily dependent on her advice, and Sadij ended up pushing her away.

Part IV

Chapter 1

After his rupture with Sandrine, Sadij began to question whether he deserved to be in a relationship; he tried to understand why he felt that way. In his innermost heart, he knew that life was too short to spend it half-hearted. On the professional level, he was doing good; however, his personal life turned out to be a real fiasco; his professional success took over his personal life.

It was a Sunday morning, Sadij was sleeping in and didn't feel like doing anything. He was lying in his bed. His eyes were closed, but his brain was well-awake. He started pondering over his desperate situation and wallowing in self-pity.

In almost all relationships I've been in, I've always taken into account my partners' feelings and even put them before mine. I sometimes have even given up the things that are important to me just to please them. Or, maybe I'm setting the bar too high. I'm probably prone to seeing all the girls I've met in a way that is without blemish, without fault and shortcoming. I've to come down to earth, after all. I have blemishes and imperfections, and perhaps I don't match up to the guy they may be looking for. Come to think of it, I don't have to regret all the failed relationships I've been through, for they may not be worth fighting for. Perhaps, the real love that will give me butterflies is yet to come!

In all relationships that Sadij had, he was more concerned with finding a partner that resembled him in terms of character traits and less concerned with coming to terms with his father's wound. The trauma of a physically and emotionally absent father had substantially affected all of his failed intimate relationships. He just didn't know how to make a relationship last. He contacted his alter ego, Jaaba, and explained to him the situation; the latter advised him to seek a therapist's counselling. He finally decided to make an appointment to see a psychiatrist.

That was the first time Sadij was sitting down in a therapist's office. As soon as the psychiatrist ordered him to come in, he kindly requested him to have a seat and gave him some paperwork to fill out. Sadij's first therapy session took place in a room that was close to the waiting room. To make Sadij feel more comfortable and protect his privacy, he had a white noise machine that he used to drown out voices. Before embarking upon asking Sadij questions, he set a timer that was to go off at the end of the session.

Then, he asked, *'How do you feel today?'*

Sadij was a bit shocked because if he were okay, the counsellor wouldn't catch him there sitting in front of him.

Sadij got his act together and said, *'Not bad, doc.'*

'Why have you decided to start counselling?' the therapist wanted to know.

Sadij vaguely explained why he was there. *'I have some personal problems.'* While Sadij was talking, the doctor was taking notes.

He requested Sadij to get to the point. *'Tell it to me like a man. What kind of personal problems are you suffering from?'*

'Look, sir. I have the utmost faith in you, and a friend of

mine advised me to consult you. I'm unable to make a relationship last. Negativity has taken over, making me unable to see the bright side of anything, to the point that I have become a merchant of doom, and I got the impression that I'm bringing the mood down wherever I go.'

'How many girls have you dated so far?' asked the therapist.

Sadij was a bit shocked because he didn't see this embarrassing question coming. He was writhing with shame and uneasiness, trying hard to control himself so that he could think about what to say appropriately. He stroked his chin, as he was asking himself whether he had to lay it on the line and thereby put his mind to rest. The doc, seeing that Sadij was a bit shy and didn't dare to open up to him, galvanised him into wearing his heart on his sleeve.

'Listen, Sadij. This is a therapeutic process that I need to make you go through. Don't be shocked if you feel you get probed to go deeper than the casual chit-chat that you're used to. This is a simple question that you have to regard as a jumping-off point for what will ensue. Right?'

Sadij nodded his assent and answered the doc's question honestly and directly.

'If my memory isn't at fault, I've dated seven girls.'

'Can you just explain to me what happens every time you try to make the relationship last?' The doctor wanted to know. That was why he expressed an insatiable curiosity, as he looked Sadij in the eye.

Sadij was now resolute to get everything off his chest; therefore, he discharged all those secrets he had been keeping to himself, and which had all along caused him so much emotional distress.

'To be frank with you, Doc, every time I like a girl and want her to be mine, she tells me she only wants to be my friend. Lately, I've been dating a girl I met on a dating application; we spent so much time together. When I suggested I want to have her more than just a friend, she said she just wants to be friends. I just can't understand why when a guy wants to take things seriously, they just back off. This has happened to me several times.'

Mr Hakim, that was the therapist's name, was listening with rapt attention to what Sadij was relating. The latter continued explaining his case.

'I just don't know what this damned thing is that turns them off. Is there something that I am doing wrong? I just don't want to spend my entire life on my own, and cast in the friend zone with the girl I want to be mine. Please help me and advise me, Doc.'

Sadij was a bit surprised to find out that he opened up more than he had expected to. He was astounded by how freely words came out of his mouth and tears welled up in his eyes.

Mr Hakim adjusted his spectacles, straightened his shirt and said, 'Let me reassure you from the get-go that, though this might seem to you to be very frustrating, at least you've managed to make some friends. Right? You can bond with all the girls. Their refusal to have a more intimate relationship is indeed disheartening. Perhaps, you may have missed the cues that they sent to tell you that they weren't interested in having you as a boyfriend. Or, maybe these girls don't feel attracted to you. They kind of feel that you're too clingy.'

When Sadij heard this painful truth, he bawled his eyes out, blubbered, boohooed, snuffled and sighed. Mr Hakim had eventually managed to lay his finger on the appropriate key that had enabled him to unlock those pent-up feelings that Sadij had been trying to suppress all along. Now, Sadij had reached a point where he felt that talking about himself was cathartic and emotionally purging. So, being in a room with his doctor had imbued Sadij with a sense of freedom to talk about himself to a person who was encouraging him to voice his thoughts plainly and bluntly.

'Now, I see that I've been defining myself through all the girls I have met, and because of their self-confidence, I have completely lost touch with who I am... er...'

Before Sadij had time to wrap up his speech, an alarm clock went off. It was the therapist's timer that signalled the end of the first session. Mr Hakim put aside the notebook wherein he was scribbling his remarks, turned to Sadij and said,

'You know within a fifty-minute session, we can't cover everything. For this first session, I've just attempted to contrive a therapeutic strategy. Don't worry if you feel you haven't said all that you had wanted to say. In later sessions, you will probably be more willing to open up. Until next session, take care of yourself, and stay well.'

Sadij felt jaded like a horse, his throat got so tickly, as he had been talking for a long time. Mr Hakim asked Sadij to get in touch with the secretary to make arrangements to schedule upcoming sessions for counselling. Now, Sadij knew when he had to come back; he then left the doctor's office and went home.

Chapter 2

Upon learning that Taib had got married and started a new life, Makiera began feeling jealous. Her feeling jealous was caused by her low self-esteem, insecurity and fear of isolation. Although she broke up with Taib a long time ago, and had no emotional connection with him, except for the only son, Sadij, they had together, Makiera had become utterly overwhelmed by that irrational feeling of jealousy. Her jealousy made little sense in as much as there was absolutely nothing to be jealous about. The reason she felt jealous was triggered by her pressing need to control Taib and make herself feel safe. Even though she was no longer his wife, nor his lover, she tried to push Taib's buttons by sending him a letter whose object was to create a very strong emotional reaction in him.

Dear Taib,
Here I am back after these two weeks of silence, my dear Taib. I think that with the start of the school year, you will certainly be very busy, but I still hope that you can answer me as soon as you can, my dear.

So I went to see Ablah to announce my decision to break up, which had to be final and unequivocal... This, as I had feared, was very painful. Ablah, although he had this behaviour that was so unpleasant to me and made me unhappy, always said that he loved me and thought he was the sweetest of men. In fact, we had never been on the same wavelength, but apparently, that didn't prevent him from being happy, despite my various attempts at separation, he had never really believed in it, and had taken our relationship for granted, never questioning his behaviour towards me. He took it as being "NORMAL". So you can't imagine how SHOCKED he was to see me so determined, so sure of myself... I cannot describe to you the sadness and disarray he immediately sank into. He was inconsolable, and it also hurt me a lot, after twenty-two years... The following days, he could not return to work, he went on emergency vacation. He only asked me for one last chance, because he said he finally understood the essential change in behaviour that he should have had and that he would henceforth have to afford an opportunity for the development of our couple. I did not want to give him this last chance because he had already had it and despite certain changes, especially on the material level, I once again experienced certain moments of suffering that I can no longer bear.

He then took tickets and paid for a trip to Turkey, in a very nice high-class tourist hotel for one week, asking me to agree to discuss this additional week again to take stock of our situation and perhaps grant him a last chance... The departure was to take place two days later, which left me very little time to decide...

Knowing that outside of Tunisia or Morocco, I had already reproached him for a long time for preventing me from traveling the world, as I had always wished, because he did not want... There he had everything he wanted to remedy this. I told him he couldn't buy me, which did upset him a lot, but it was really, he said, to take stock of the situation in a neutral, pleasant and serene setting. Despite my final decision, given the state in which he was, and considering my children, who later could also reproach me for having refused this last chance to their father, and let alone the little time that remained for me to think, I agreed to go.

During this week in Izmir, I was able to openly enumerate to him all his Achilles' heels, our having a different view of things, all the suffering that I had endured and finally that he had to accept the final separation. Obviously, he tried to go for broke, and asked me to forgive him, and apologised for everything he had done...

That he was blind and hadn't understood the situation I was going through. That I had to give him a very last chance to prove his love and good behaviour forever. That if I happened to notice the slightest deviation from the commitments he had given me today, then he would be the first to tell me, 'Okay, I failed, you have the right to leave me.' Besides, he had told me that there was no urgent need to divorce immediately and that twenty-two years of marriage deserved and required further reflection... He still has some arguments that make me say to him, okay I will make my decision in one or two weeks right after our return to France to tell you whether I will give you one last chance.

We returned from our trip to Turkey five days ago; he resumed his work on Monday. He has started to review all his behaviour and his choices and projects in favour of a reconstruction of the couple, he is hopeful and is doing all he can to turn things around. I have as much trouble seeing his efforts as I have told myself that he could have done all this long before. What was important to me was so secondary to him, and he said he was unaware of all of this.

My very dear Taib, I think all these stories of mine and all these incessant eddies are doing your head in. I feel propelled into a vortex from which there seemed to be no escape. I'm afraid of the guilt that might come over me later, and at the same time, I tell myself that I have never taken such a big step to back off now. Maybe you will be disappointed with what you've just read, but please try to understand me, your listening and your support do me so much good. I'm sorry, but whatever you think, my dear Taib, please do tell me; it helps me think and clarify my ideas. Your analysis of the situation can only help me, even if it is a negative attitude towards me, it will remain constructive for me. It's been a long time since I read your last message, what do you think? As regards Sadij, have you heard from him lately or not? I don't know. I just wish he didn't know right now that we write to each other regularly, or that I'm in touch with you, please. He is currently in Macedonia, on vacation. He is still very angry with me. I have to leave you, for now, but looking forward to reading from you very shortly. I wish you a very good start to the school year, a lot of courage and patience, Allah is always with the patients.

I wish you happiness Insha Allah. Peace and health.

Makiera

Chapter 3

As usual, whenever Taib got back from work, he logged in to check the mailbox of his email address to see if there was any message sent to him. That morning, he had been running a tutorial at university about how to analyse a novel for two hours at a stretch. Very lately, he had been burning the candles at both ends because of doing too many things and working too much; if he didn't alter his schedule, he would send himself to an early grave. After having his lunch, the only thing he wanted to do was to take a nap; so, it wasn't until late in the evening that he checked his email. Much to his surprise, he came across Makiera's long message.

Curiously enough, he read the message so many times that certain specific turns of phrases used by Makiera got deeply etched in his mind. He became overwhelmed by confusion, for his usual level of clarity to think was undermined; he was in a quandary about whether to respond to Makiera straightaway or put off answering the letter. Naturally, Taib did read between the lines of her letter and swiftly detected her hidden scheme. Taib instantly realised that she hadn't changed a bit; she had remained the same manipulative woman he knew years ago.

He started pondering over Makiera's enduring habit of lying and scheming. *I don't think she did manage to draw a lesson from her past mistakes; I'm just wondering why she's telling me all this, her trip to Izmir with Ablah, her uncertainty as to whether to stay with him or leave. I guess she's simply stirring the pot, hoping that I'll get upset. This is insane. She's doing this because she's trying to get the love and attention she needs, and that's all. We're divorced and have no emotional connections, so why should I be jealous?*

Eventually, it dawned upon Taib that Makiera was insecure, anxious, dreaded ending up being alone and there was virtually no support out there to allay her fears of abandonment; therefore, the following day, he decided to comfort her with his soothing and wise advice. He then sat at a table, took a pen and a paper and began to write.

Hello, dear Makiera,

I hope these few lines will do you good. You know, dear Makiera, I didn't answer you right away because I honestly didn't know what to tell you at the time. I was really confused, and I wouldn't want your judgments, evaluations and decisions to be influenced by my advice. All I wish from the bottom of my heart is to see you happy Insha Allah. You can't imagine how sad and helpless I feel for not being able to alleviate your pain. Your pain is mine, and above all keep in mind that I will always be there for you. Mostly, I don't want you to feel like I don't feel what you feel. Try not to let this feeling of isolation turn into a vicious cycle. Have confidence in yourself because I know that you will, Insha Allah, get out of the woods. Do not let sorrow take away your ability to enjoy life, for sorrow and grief are bad things from which a believer must stay away. I have read your message very carefully and many times, and I understand how you feel, my dear Makiera. All this time, I've been thinking about the difficult time you are going through, my dear Makiera. All my prayers, all my heart, all my mind and all of my being are with you. I apologise if I can't find the right words with which to comfort you. I am, just like you, very confused, believe me; I haven't stopped thinking about what support, advice or help I can provide you with to help you overcome these difficult times for you and me too, because I have to remind you that your sufferings are mine, and I will never let you down; I will always be there for you, and I will spare no effort to support you. My support for you is and will always remain unconditional. The only and effective advice I can suggest is to perform the prayer of seeking Allah's guidance. This prayer allows us to consult Allah before making a decision and thus, to avoid certain mistakes. It allows us to ask Allah to guide us in our choices; believe me, dear Makiera, nothing is more efficient than showing one's need for the Almighty's constant help and inordinate grace.

And believe me, dear Makiera, that if what you want to do is facilitated by Allah, continue, but if you see signs that suggest that the course of what you want to do is strewn with pitfalls, then let go. It is better to perform this prayer before going to bed. May Allah assist you, my dearest Makiera. But most of all, remember that I am and always will be there for you. And if you want to confide in me or directly consult with me, you can reach me by phone.

I just want to see you happy in your life.

Chapter 4

While Sadij was getting some counselling from Dr Hakim to improve his psychological health, his mother, Makiera, was abandoned by all her children, and before her children discovered that she was a toxic and manipulative mother, the words alienation and estrangement had never been part of her vocabulary. Her feeling incredibly lonely was an expected fallout from their realisation that she had been good at twisting the truth to make herself look good and to paint her husband as the villain. Playing the victim card had pushed her children, her friends, even her fellow workers away. Now that she was forsaken, with no one to console her or alleviate her grief, she engaged in bemoaning her fate.

I've never imagined that one day all my sons will cut me out of their lives. How could they do this to me? I'm the one that gave them life, love, affection and a safe shelter. I've never thought that one day they will stab me in the back! Now, it did happen, and here I'm on my own, all the sacrifices I made have simply gone up in smoke. Never in my life have I felt so worthless and unwanted as I do now.

To purge her distress, she started crying, covering her face with her hands. A crestfallen Makiera didn't know how to cope with being ditched by everyone. But there remained that flicker of hope that she clung to. And that was her saviour, Taib. She then took a pen and a paper and started writing a letter to him.

Dear Taib,

I hope you're doing pretty fine. I'm getting worried, for it's been a long time since I heard from you. Also, I heard that in Morocco, COVID-19 is wreaking havoc on all levels, especially in Marrakech where the death toll is rising very dramatically. You don't know how precious your presence and our correspondence are to me. Moreover, in these difficult moments that I am going through now, you are my guarantee of being better, the conscience that I may be missing and the reliable, wise and reassuring person who allows me to find happiness in everyday living. I have the impression of being a weather vane that turns in circles, and which despite its seemingly strong decisions, takes a huge step back by falling back into the abyss of dismalness. All my children have lately turned against me. At this moment, your son, Sadij, is against me too, I have never imagined I could get to where I am now. Everything can change so quickly and so unexpectedly. Soon I may end up finding myself alone at my age and to continue life alone; one must at least have the support and presence of one's children. Being alone doesn't bother me if I find peace and serenity, but I need to keep the love and trust of my children.

You know, Taib, if you have no objection to our continuing our correspondence, and if you don't mind continuing to do my heart good, and lift my spirits every time I read you, then it is MORE THAN ENOUGH for my wellbeing.

Still causing harm to your relationship is the furthest thing from my mind. All I'm asking is to be able to count on your presence that is so wise, so pious, full of kindness and reassuring for me.

*Please let me know what you're up to, as soon as you can,
at least to reassure me about your wellbeing.*

I only want your happiness.

Makiera

That afternoon, Taib was in his office at the University of Cadi
Ayyad, holding a meeting with his research students
administering the final touches to their monographs. As soon
as the meeting came to an end, Taib checked his mailbox for
new messages, and there staring him in the face was Makiera's
message. He read it slowly and thoroughly, making out what's
being said, and making valuable connections between what he
already knew about his ex-wife and the new things he was
learning about her now. The first thing which struck Taib
above all else was her sudden and unexpected show of concern
for Taib's state of health. Taib was intrigued by this sudden
personality change in his ex-wife; what happened to that one-
time uncouth and unfeeling woman to become such a tender-
hearted and loving creature? Taib started fretting about that
dramatic change in Makiera's opinions and feelings. He could
still remember how she used to be so callous and hard- hearted
with him.

Therefore, he sat still in his office chair wondering about
what brought about such a personality change in her. He
eventually realised that that mood swing was due to those
upsetting life events that she had been through, especially her
divorce from Ablah and her being estranged from all her
children. She was depressed and left in the dark trying to figure
out what went wrong. That gut-wrenching experience she was
undergoing began to trouble Taib very seriously. Now, he had
the unshakable premonition that she might take to drugs,

alcohol or even worse; take her own life. So, he firmly believed that her state of mind required immediate attention; besides, the note with which she rounded off her message signalled her earnest appeal to his support and sympathy. Therefore, Taib was convinced that his support and encouragement would certainly play a key role in Makiera's recovery. He also felt guilty and responsible for her depression. He then started responding to her message without any further delay.

Hello, dear and adorable Makiera,

Writing to someone who is very dear to us is not only an enormous pleasure but an immense joy as well. And you don't have to thank me because I haven't done anything yet to deserve your thanks, my very dear and adorable Makiera, and I can't wait to redeem myself, to make you forget all these pains that are, at the end of the day, nothing else by fleeting clouds; just let me make amends for the anguish I caused you by filling your heart with joy, Insha Allah. And believe me that all these words that you qualify as tender, sweet and deep do emanate from a big heart with much love in it because hatred is a feeling that can only exist in the absence of intelligence. To hear you say that my words give you the strength to face up to the daily challenges of life does me a lot of good, but to me, they remain just words, as long as they are not translated into actions. You know, my dear Makiera, you can turn to me, because I am the person most able to give you a helping hand. If you feel like talking it out to get a solution to a problem, I will always be there for you. How can't one be fully attentive to the person that is very dear to him? Putting oneself in the shoes of others and feeling their suffering is the hallmark of a human being's goodness.

Listening to you, my dear and beloved Makiera, does me a lot of good. I'm not one of those who have their heads in the clouds or a little self-centred. However, I have my flaws. A wise man is someone ashamed of his faults but is not ashamed of mending his ways, and the biggest flaw is to ignore one's defects. You can confide in me. You know that you are not going to bother me at all with everything you're gonna tell me; on the contrary, I would like to do a lot of good things for you. I want to know what your needs are, my dear Makiera, and I am ready to meet them at all costs. You need to know that I understand you more than anyone, and that I will accept whatever comes from you because you mean a lot to me, and that all the suffering we endured together could have been avoided. Believe me, I keep blaming myself whenever I think about it. I am and will always be there for you. I understand you, I support you and I will always support you no matter what. All I want is your happiness. It hurts me a lot to feel that you are in pain, believe me.

I want to help you at all costs. I don't want you to feel that I'm bothering you or that I'm poking my nose into your own business because to me your business and your problems are mine.

Take care of yourself and keep in mind that I am always there for you

Taib, who only wants to see you happy in this life.

May Allah (Glorified and Exalted Be He) assist you in whatever you set out to do!

May good luck and success always be by your side, Insha ALLAH!

Chapter 5

Today, Sadij had an appointment with his therapist; it was the second healing session that he had to go through to develop his self-esteem and enhance future lasting intimate and emotional attachments. After he had had his breakfast, he went up to see Doc. Hakim. He took the subway and a bus to get to the psychiatrist's office. When he arrived, he found Mr Hakim very busy with one of his patients; therefore, he had to wait for more than an hour. To while the time away, he took a magazine that was lying on a table, leafed through it and came across an article that read, *"Healing the Past"*. He went about perusing the article with rapt attention, acting as an avid bookworm. He was so engrossed in the purport of the article that he didn't hear the doctor's secretary call his name.

The young and blonde medical secretary, seeing that Sadij was miles away, came up to him, and said, *'Sir, it's your turn, and the doctor is waiting for you.'*

As soon as he heard these words, he sprang to his feet and made for the door. And there was sitting at his desk Mr Hakim. The instant he caught sight of Sadij, he greeted him and requested him to sit on a chair facing him.

Mr Hakim launched the conversation, saying, *'Well, last time, we talked a bit about yourself. Today, I would like to know more about your family. I mean your parents. Your relationship with your mum and dad. Introduce me vicariously*

to your father and your mother. Tell me more about your
relationship with both of them.'

As soon as the therapist tried to probe into the nature of
the relationship Sadij had with both his mother and father,
Sadij became overwhelmed by a very strong feeling of
resentment and sadness. In his case, Sadij felt abandoned by
both Taib and Makiera. His father walked away when Sadij
was only five years old, but the one question that he was
struggling with was why did his father leave him? And now
that the doctor asked him to describe the kind of relationship
he was having with his parents, he felt ill at ease; how he
wished he hadn't come to see the therapist. How he wished he
could disappear. He was overcome by a sudden and
uncontrolled feeling that told him to get up and leave the
therapist's medical office. He experienced some discomfort,
especially when he realised that the doc's inquiry into his
relationship with his parents was a done deal, as there was no
way around it. He felt ashamed, touched the side of his
forehead, blocked his eyes, held a notepad that was on the
doc's desk and didn't seem to be ready to open up to Mr
Hakim. He covered his mouth as if he was trying to keep
something from Mr Hakim.

The latter immediately spotted Sadij's attempt at dodging
the issue, pushed the envelope of Sadij's discretion a bit further
and reformulated his request,

'If I ask you to rate your relationship with your father,
what would be your appraisal? Using the following words:
bad, good and excellent.'

Sadij had had the experience of being questioned about
the whereabouts of his father when he was young. At the time,
he used to say that his father passed away to ward off people's

potential disgraceful gossip about his private life. But this time, the reason he didn't want to respond to Mr Hakim's question was that the point at issue now was somewhat inappropriate, and went over a personal boundary. However, upon quick reflection, he became fully conscious of the fact that his therapist had the right to know everything about him if he ever wished to get over his relationship insecurity. He, therefore, poised himself for the anguish that would follow from this touchy and personal question. At no time in his entire life had he ever felt loved and emotionally attached to his parents. He steadied himself on the arm of the chair, cleared his throat and began to open up about his childhood emotional neglect.

'The biggest riddle of my life, Doc, is trying to figure out why my dad left when I just turned five. According to my mother, he has never wanted children. Then soon after that, my mother decided to start a new life with another man. And I feel as if I was an unwanted child. My mum has never told me to reconnect with him. She was twenty-five and my father twenty-seven when I was born. They had been married for almost four years, rented an apartment in Creteil. My father was still pursuing his postgraduate studies at Sorbonne University, and my mother didn't have a regular job at the time. My father had never wanted to have children because of all the commitments that a family life entailed. My dad had never been a presence in my life. All along, I've been wondering why he left me, and why he didn't love me. The vacuity that his absence left in my life seemed just like a deep abyss that's hard to fill. I'm still wondering what made him choose to walk out of my life. When I asked my mother what made my dad abandon me, she callously replied that he just didn't want me to be in his life.

Honestly, Doc, it was only recently that I realised that my mother has never been straightforward with me about the facts, because lately she split up with my stepfather and tried to convince me to reconnect with my father. When I asked her what made her change her mind, she said that Dad is a good and honest man.'

Mr Hakim, seeing that Sadij was getting out of breath, asked his secretary to bring a water bottle, because Sadij's throat got so tickly, as he had been talking for a long period. He took the bottle and gulped all the water down. He felt as though he had a frog in his throat, for he was unable to speak, and his throat was sore. Mr Hakim, in an attempt to allay the excruciating pain that Sadij was feeling as a result of getting those pent-up feelings off his chest, began to speak.

'Listen, Mr Sadij, whatever reason your father had for leaving, you have to know that there's absolutely nothing that you did to push your father to go away. And there's nothing either that you could do to prevent him from leaving. And there's nothing you could have done to make both of your parents love you more; and there's nothing you did to make them hate you. One thing you need to remember all the time is that you're not responsible for what happened, and you're neither responsible for your parents' actions. Just tell me, Mr Sadij, did your father grow up without a father himself?'

Sadij was caught on the hop by Mr Hakim's unexpected question; he felt confused because the therapist turned the conversation into a touchy topic that left Sadij feeling bad about himself; the therapist's client was mentally unprepared to cope with the question; his eyes were darting around, and his head turning, as if he was searching for an answer. Scratching his left cheek and rubbing his chin. Mr Hakim couldn't understand what it was that he had said that made Sadij feel so rattled and disconcerted. He then tried to reformulate his question.

'*The point is more often than not most fathers that choose to abandon their families have experienced significant harm in their own lives; this is just a conjecture... I mean they may have undergone a certain trauma in their childhood and are afraid that they might harm their offspring in the same way. So, I just want to know whether your father did grow up without a father himself.*'

Convinced that he had nothing to lose, Sadij walked into the lion's den of his therapist's inquiry, looked him in the eye, and started telling the whole truth.

'*Honestly, Doc, my father did grow up without a father himself.*'

Mr Hakim said, '*I see. As I said early on, you're not to blame for all of that. But, and this is what I want you to pay close attention to, the physical and emotional absence of a father may engender bouts of depression and introversion. Does it ever happen to you to feel that you're all alone in this world and that nobody can understand what you're feeling? Isn't that so?*' Sadij nodded his head in agreement. The therapist continued his inquiry. '*Tell me, Mr Sadij, you more often tend to be aggressive and quick to anger. Right?*'

Sadij agreed and commented, '*Personally, Doc, I've always had a huge amount of anger, but just quiet anger. I've always tried to contain the rage... that unretractable monster that's been building up inside of me. I've always said to myself that it's immature and socially unacceptable to outwardly show one's anger, and that one just looks like a kid when one fails to control one's anger. After all, Doc, anger makes one act stupidly.'*

Mr Hakim cast a glance at his timer, turned to his client and said, *'Well, the time allotted to today's session is up. We will continue this next time. Just check with the secretary so that she can fit you into my schedule next week. Okay? Take care and catch you next time.'*

Sadij stood up and did make like a tree and left.

Chapter 6

Makiera's dream of founding a large family and having a loving husband had collapsed, leaving her with no option but to take advantage of Taib's kindness; having lost control of her life and gone to the dogs, she thought that Taib was the best alternative that could help her feel in control. To achieve her malignant aims and unmet needs with the least effort, she attempted to control Taib's life, using sadistic means to restore her mental balance, calm down her insecurities and accordingly feel better about herself. Therefore, she decided to travel to Morocco to meet up with her first husband. She belatedly realised how stupid she had been to have let Taib slip through her fingers; now she was more determined than ever before to engage in stealing Taib from his wife. She tried to lure him away from Malak.

As soon as Makiera arrived at Marrakesh Menara airport, she gave Taib a buzz, telling him that she would be staying at Dar Bahi guest house in the old medina. Since Taib was a very kind and tender-hearted man, he always prioritised others' feelings over his; owing to the letters that Makiera had sent him, he inadvertently stepped into her shoes, reconstructed in his own mind's eye the anguish she was experiencing. The very idea of having a son with her itself swiftly impelled him to tune in to her sufferings. Before going to the guest house where Makiera was staying, Taib informed his wife, Malak, about it, because he had never felt the need to hide anything from his wife. For him, marriage had always been a very solid bond based on honesty, honour, integrity and commitment; therefore, in a marital relationship, there was no room for lies, deceit and cheating, for he had always and firmly believed that lying just gave a man's wife a good reason to lose faith in him, and that if that trust was broken, it would be next to impossible to restore it.

He drove to Dar Bahi guest house in the old medina. When Taib arrived, he went straight to the front desk and asked the receptionist, *'Excuse me, sir, I'm looking for a lady who has just checked in. Her name's Makiera and is from Paris.'*

The young man behind the counter was very friendly and helpful; he immediately checked the hotel guest book to make sure the name of the lady was there and said, *'She's in room sixty-nine, sir.'*

Taib then requested the receptionist to inform her about his arrival. A few minutes later, Makiera joined Taib in the lobby and led him to a nearby patio with a very wonderful fountain in the middle; at the other end of that roofless inner courtyard, there was a very large living room with a fireplace. She then beckoned to a waiter, who came over to them.

'Good morning, Madame. How can I help you?' the gentleman asked politely.

Makiera ordered an orange juice, Taib requested to be supplied with herbal tea, and they chatted for a while. Now, Taib was all hers, she said to herself, casting furtive glances at him now and then. She vehemently hoped that her scheming and dirty tricks might work their charms on him. To get Taib's attention, Makiera played up her great rack by wearing a dress that showed some of her cleavage, thus causing Taib feelings of acute embarrassment. Makiera was so interested in having Taib completely obsessed with her that she made use of all flirting and seduction techniques available to seduce him. Taib immediately spotted that she was up to her old tricks again. She said, *It's really good to see you again. I miss you, and can't wait to be close to you. You know despite the distance that separates us, you're always in my mind; there's not a single that day that goes by without me missing you. Tell me, dear Taib...'*

She held his hand, and pressed it gently. Taib was really disconcerted by the waiter, who waited upon them, and was within a very short distance to see what was going on. Makiera, however, was too well into her game that she brazened the whole thing out with impudent self-confidence. It dawned upon Taib that Makiera had come to Marrakech to destroy his robust relationship with Malak. Makiera did mistakenly believe that Taib had gotten too comfortable with his wife that he had fallen into a routine that engendered boredom. Taib realised that being nice entailed a lot of pitfalls; therefore, he remained nice and compassionate towards his ex-wife while maintaining his boundaries.

'You're a nice woman, and I understand that you're going through a rough patch at the moment. I'm sorry but I can't help you out this time. You know I'm a married guy, and it doesn't do to...' He had no sooner finished his statement than he was butted in by Makiera, who stood up to leave.

'I deduced from the letters that we exchanged that you wanted to have me back in your life. How silly I was...' She broke down in tears and started blubbering.

Taib rose to his feet too and tried to console her. *'I do feel your disappointment.'*

He felt as if he was being held hostage by Makiera's emotional needs. How he wished he could attend to her needs without sacrificing his own, and screwing up his own life. He didn't expect that by putting himself in her shoes, he would find it hard, later on, to extricate himself from the empathy trap he was hemmed in. Makiera continued to play the victim, appearing sincere, but that was just a facade that covered her malignant intentions. The only thing she was hankering after at the moment was to lure Taib away from his wife, Malak. Taib knew now and without a doubt that Makiera was a selfish and ungrateful woman whose main concern was to take advantage of his kindness. Indeed, Makiera was ready to go to any length to just exploit and manipulate Taib to serve her own needs, and Taib turned out to be the easiest target. Makiera got more and more worried, as she felt that she was beginning to lose ground in her bid to win Taib over. She then started telling lies to disguise her true manipulative nature and true colours.

'You perfectly know that your son has recently turned his back on me, and refused to talk to me, his mother, after all the tremendous sacrifices I've made. I brought him up on my own, and now he's letting me down. I don't deserve to be treated that way. Do I? If you hadn't walked out on us, we would never have been where we are today.'

She attempted to make him believe that he was the one that had caused the problem that she had begun, but was unwilling to take responsibility for; she immediately started crying, throwing herself into Taib's arms to test his readiness to go the extra mile to help her. Taib realised that being kind didn't mean that he had to be a weak target. He, therefore, decided to bring Makiera to reason.

'Listen, Makiera, what's done cannot be undone. You

know as well as I do that I'm not to blame. So, let's stop blaming each other, 'cause this won't change anything between us. Just for the sake of old acquaintance, let's remain friends and reconnect with our son, Sadij, to help him overcome his lack of self-assurance so that he may have successful relationships in the future.'

Makiera, at first, had believed she had a chance of drawing Taib in and ensnaring him in an illicit relationship because he was a very kind and caring man that wanted to help. That was why she had tried through the agency of her messages to prey on his emotional sensitivity and scrupulous conscientiousness. Even now, Taib could remember how she used to praise in the messages she had sent his goodness and kindness. But now that she was unable to secure what she wanted, she became extremely aggressive, vicious and unwilling to let go until she wore Taib down. She was out of her skull, shouting out at Taib, who was extremely embarrassed because all the people that were sitting in that roofless inner courtyard kept looking and wondering what was going on. Taib, who could no longer bear all the eyes that were focused on him, ran like the wind down the patio and walked out of the guest house.

Chapter 7

Once in her room, she called room service for George Killian's Irish red beer. Before the young waiter came up to her room, she swiftly applied some mascara on her eyes to entice him and get him wild with her searching eyes. She wore an extremely short skirt and a push-up bra. As soon as the bloke rapped at the door, Makiera opened the door, exposing large areas of her breasts and allowing the guy to take a sneak peek now and then. The young man was a bit embarrassed, but Makiera gave him a seductive smile, and after the manner of a very experienced flirtatious woman, she turned back and leaned forward to pick some tips from her bag, giving the bloke the god-send opportunity to take a closer look at her voluptuous butt. The young man immediately realised that she was throwing herself at him, ignored her, snatched the tip, took to his heels and Makiera ended up looking cheap and desperate. She spent the whole night on her own, drowning in her sorrows.

The next day, she woke up in her bed with that empty bottle of beer lying close by. She felt like she had a hangover; she could remember what happened and was accordingly overcome by a spurious sense of shame. She eventually curtailed her stay and went back to Paris. Makiera's failed attempt at taking Taib from his family, from his wife, from his daughters and his safe home taught her that pure love was not about how manipulative she could be, how sexy and enticing she was; there was more to it than that. The most important thing that Makiera had overlooked all her life was that real love was an ineffable, ethereal sensation that could awaken a person's soul. And even now, and in the face of hard and overwhelming evidence, she kept pushing back against the irrefutable truth, unwilling to admit she had been wrong in any circumstance, refusing to accept full responsibility for all the clumsy and stupid mistakes she had made in her life. Therefore, at this very moment, her brittle ego urged her to utterly distort her perception of what had happened that night at Dar Bahi guest house in Marrakech to make that disruptive and unhappy incident seem trivial; she now felt that she was no longer wrong or guilty of anything.

Whereupon, she called her son Sadij because she felt lonely and there was no one around to talk to. She feared that she might sink into a state of dejection and tension as a result of her apprehension of remaining all by herself for the rest of her life. She kept calling her son, but it just went straight to the voice mail. Her feeling lonely got more and more poignant; it even led her to rumination. She began wallowing in self-pity.

'Why am I alone? What did I do to deserve what's happening to me?'

It was very hard for her to realise that she ought to have rather been a self-pitying person in regards to her dereliction of duty in all the things that had befallen her. Instead, she kept constantly mulling over problems, feeling gloomy and despondent because of what she thought life had dealt her. And now more than ever before, she was desperately in need of the compassion and commiseration of her relatives and children.

Nevertheless, Makiera had made of that exacerbated sense

of pity over her miserable life a toxic habit, thus alienating all the people she needed now from her. Feeling being left in the lurch, and having no one to turn to for help, she indulged in excessive drinking and binge eating to assuage her suffering. And when misfortunes happened, they tended to follow each other in rapid succession. So, the tidings of the death of Makiera's mother, Mrs Moukafiha, came like a bolt from the blue, triggering some psychiatric disorders in Makiera, who had become addicted to alcohol; her drinking problem compromised her job, for she started neglecting her responsibilities at work, in the hospital where she had been working for more than twenty years now, thus jeopardising her career. She then started living on the dole and receiving charity from the French government. With that small governmental allowance, she was unable to keep a roof over her head and was ousted from her abode. Now, she became homeless, and it was a very cold and snowy November in Paris. Luckily for her, she was given an emergency shelter by an association in Paris. She was entitled to bed and breakfast. As soon as she took breakfast, the refectory closed, and Makiera found herself rooming and wandering from one subway station to another, killing time by drinking some cheap beers and wine.

Chapter 8

While Makiera was boozing herself to death and rubbing shoulders with the homeless in the famous streets of Paris, Sadij was having his third session with his therapist. Unlike the first and second sessions wherein Mr Hakim tried to establish a rapport with Sadij that was based on trust to impel the latter to open up to him, this third encounter consisted in identifying the best course of action that Sadij ought to take to move towards change and reconcile with the past. It was Mr Hakim who was calling the shots this time.

'Read my lips, Mr Sadij. If you want to cope successfully with that lack of self-assurance that's constantly causing a lot of problems in your relationships, you need to heal your past. You have to break this cycle of anguish by making peace with your past. Otherwise, your wounded past would become a generational issue. Get my drift?'

Sadij didn't seem to catch on to what Mr Hakim was trying to get across to him; he then replied, *'I don't know where you're coming from, sir.'*

The therapist attempted to recast his message differently, *'The point is, if you're not ready to embark on a healing journey that consists in coming to grips with that emotional void that you've been suffering from since you were five, then you will never be able to create lasting love with your prospective partners. I mean you need to make an effort to understand, accept and deal with that if you aspire to allow yourself to grow in the future. And the worst-case scenario that we all wish would never happen is to repeat the same mistake that your parents made.'*

Sadij seemed like he just wasn't listening. He was wondering about how that bleak past of his would affect his ability to have a successful relationship with any girl. Mr Hakim kept watching him, trying to read his facial expressions to sense how he felt. Exhausted and exasperated, Sadij, who was at the end of his tether, wanted to know what goddamned thing was it that needed modification and that he had long been protecting.

'Tell me, Doc, what has my past got to do with my relationships? I just... I don't... I don't see the connection.'

Mr Hakim's face brightened as if Sadij had hit the target. *'Bingo! you're right on target. We're now making good progress. Let's call a spade a spade and acknowledge that the physical and emotional absence of your father in your life is just like a vacant space that's been created inside of you and that needs to fill so that you may not have to bear the consequences of this void. Right?'*

Sadij remained silent, numb and listened with rapt attention to Mr Hakim's explanation.

'And that empty space that's within you needs to be filled with affection and unconditional love. What kids need most is the emotional support that's supplied by parents. And this is something that we human beings desperately need in our lives, something we can never do without; so, when we grow up without that emotional prop, we feel like we do lack an essential ingredient for which there's no substitute. Dig?'

Sadij nodded in agreement.

Mr Hakim looked Sadij in the eye and asked him, *'Tell me, how do you feel whenever the name of your father is mentioned in a conversation? Pray, do answer my question honestly.'*

Sadij steadied himself in the chair, stroked his chin, and said, *'You want a sincere answer, Doc?'*

'Of course!' replied the therapist.

Without any further hesitation, Sadij spoke his piece, *'All right, let me tell it like it is. I feel resentment and anger towards him. I will never forgive his letting me down when I was desperately in need of him. I promise I will never do that to my kids if ever I get married and have some.'*

Mr Hakim looked at his timer and said, *'Well said, but you need to rid yourself of that grudge that you bear against your father first because if you don't, you will always end up breaking up with your potential partners. Well... I think that's enough for today. We will continue this healing journey next time. Take care and stay well.'*

'Have a nice day, Doc,' replied Sadij, who was holding a leather jacket in his hand. He then went away without scheduling any upcoming appointment with the therapist's secretary.

Chapter 9

That emotional neglect that Sadij had been the victim of throughout his childhood had left indelible marks on his personality, for he continued to be unable to create and strike lasting emotional bonds with the opposite sex. He had a bee in his bonnet about the motives that had induced his father to walk away.

Did he choose to abandon me of his own free accord? Or, was he compelled to? That was the most mind-boggling conundrum that he had failed to decipher so far. How he wished he could meet his father and clear up that mystery! But every time he attempted to move forward, something else kept holding him back, and that was that inexorable and deep-seated rancour that kept devouring him from within. He was completely immersed in his thoughts, when he suddenly received a call from his Aunt Moutalaiba, informing him that his mother was brought to the emergency room after attempting to take her own life by taking pills.

Distraught, he went straight to the hospital where the emergency staff asked him why he was there.

He replied, *'My mother has just been admitted to hospital… er…'*

Sadij was very worried and upset, and couldn't feel his leg. He would have fallen in a swoon were it not for the fact that two nurses happened to be there at that moment. One of the nurses sat and placed Sadij's head between her knees; the other one lifted his legs above heart level to aid blood flow to his brain. She then loosened the collar of his shirt and the belt of his trousers.

A few seconds later, he regained consciousness and was about to stand up when one of the nurses ordered him to rest; she then requested one of her colleagues to bring candy or something sweet for Sadij to suck on to help raise his blood sugar levels. They took him to a nearby room to take an x-ray to make sure that he had no unusual muscle spasms. After close examination, it turned out that he was out of harm's way.

Sadij asked one of the radiographers that had carried out the x-ray, *'I'm here to see my mother who was admitted to hospital this morning. Her name is Mrs Makiera. Will you please help me?'*

The radiographer, a silver-haired man in his mid-fifties and with a big moustache, smiled at him and said, *'Of course! We will take you to the emergency service that's in charge of admitting patients.'*

With great alacrity, Sadij grabbed the man's hand and gratefully thanked him. Whereupon came a primary care physician who was in charge of dealing with suicidal patients.

'You're the patient's son, aren't you?' the man asked Sadij.

The latter answered, *'Yeah, sir.'*

The primary care physician went on explaining the strategy that he was going to adopt. *'The first thing that we need to do is to stabilise your mother's state and ensure her medical safety. Then, a thorough assessment of her suicide attempt will be made, together with in-depth scrutiny of the probability of recurrence of this. Right?'*

Sadij was extremely shocked, and the only words that

could come out of his mouth were, *'I see.'*

The doctor continued his speech in a very earnest tone, *'I just want you to answer some of my questions if you don't mind.'*

The mental health crisis professional was waiting for Sadij's cooperation, but the latter was flabbergasted and struck dumb; he then went on explaining, *'The thing is, we need to evaluate your mother's mental health crisis to determine the appropriate help that she needs and that suits her situation before referring her to a specialist.'*

Eventually, Sadij realised that he had to be honest and cooperate; sweating like hell, with his legs still stiff, he had to support himself by leaning against the wall.

He gradually pulled himself together and began to speak appropriately, *'Go ahead, sir, and ask me any questions! I'm ready to do anything to help my mother get out of this.'*

The doc seemed to be very delighted with Sadij's readiness to help. *'It is really good to hear you say this. Now, tell me, er... sorry to have taken the liberty to talk to you without first asking what your name is.'*

Sadij told him his name, and the primary care physician embarked upon asking Makiera's son an array of questions. *'Has your mother ever thought about suicide before, or tried to harm herself before?'*

Sadij answered in a very tense and self-assured tone, *'Not as far as I know, Doc.'*

The doctor asked Sadij, *'Are you aware of the fact that your mother did take some pills to take her life?'*

Dumfounded, Sadij couldn't believe what he heard. Worse, he had more surprises to come, for the doctor informed him that Makiera was addicted to alcohol and that she had become a vagrant wandering from place to place. When Sadij heard this staggering piece of news, he burst into tears. The doctor tried to comfort him, reassuring him that special attention would be given to her case and that she would be transferred first to a detoxification centre where she was going to undergo a recovery program.

Chapter 10

By dint of being addicted to alcohol, Makiera's body had become used to having alcohol in her blood system; to remove all traces of alcohol from her body, she was placed in an appropriate treatment setting in Marmottan Hospital in Paris. During her detox process, she was deprived of alcohol, which led to some withdrawal symptoms. She felt the world spinning around her, giving her the intractable desire to vomit; she spent one whole night going back and forth between her room and the restroom, soiling the hall between the two spaces. As a result of months of heavy drinking, she had developed acute fits of fatal delirium. One day, she started acting in a very peculiar way in that she broke a glass, took a small piece of it and began tearing up her mattress and screaming in a shrill voice. When an asylum nurse tried to prevent her from ripping up her bed, Makiera put her hands around the nurse's neck and choked her. Makiera was so strong that she lifted the young lady's body off the ground and were it not for the shrill and loud cries that the young lady made, she would have kicked the bucket.

Upon hearing those high-pitched and piercing sounds of entreaty, three nurses rushed to the rescue of their colleague. All of a sudden, Makiera found herself hemmed in on all sides by the three nurses, who swiftly put her in a straitjacket to restrain her violent behaviour. As she could no longer use physical force, because her arms were tightly bound against her body, she resorted to verbal abuse.

'If I catch you... you... you dirty sluts, I will kill you.'

The nurses were angry, but they just listened and tried to understand what was wrong with the patient. Seeing that her strategy didn't work out as she had hoped, she then tried to make them feel guilty and position herself as the victim.

'Because I'm a helpless and lonely woman, you took advantage of me.'

Afterward, she burst into tears, yelling and shouting out with all her might. The services of the chief nursing officer were immediately sought. And there came along the corridor a tall, handsome chief nurse executive with a syringe in his hand; he inserted the needle into her left hand and injected a dose of morphine to allay Makiera's unruly irascibility. Notwithstanding the use of physical restraint and constant medication to curb Makiera's intimidating aggression, she went on with her hostile behaviour and unrelenting physical assaults, causing serious injury to other patients and staff members. The hospital management decided to involve a psychiatrist.

Chapter 11

Following her serious and repeated acts of aggression, Makiera was excluded from certain services to which patients were entitled. She tended towards forgetfulness and got more and more disoriented, thinking she was in a place and time she was not in; she started to see things and got more and more paranoid, thinking that all the nurses in the hospital were going to hurt her. One day, her sister, Moutalaiba paid her a short visit. When Makiera caught sight of her sister, she called her by another woman's name.

'Sarah! it's really... good to see you!'

Her failing to recognise her sister did upset Moutalaiba, who found it baffling and annoying to try to remind her sister of who she was.

A few minutes later, Makiera's attending physician took Moutalaiba aside and tried to explain to her the sensitivity and specificity of her sister's case.

'At this point, it's very important to keep connections with her. You know... eh... your sister is suffering from dementia and is desperately in need of you. You know, remembering faces and names does come and go. So, you don't have to worry if she doesn't recognise you for the first time.'

Moutalaiba was held spellbound by the doctor's explanation. Lulled to sleep by the doctor's tedious elocution, Moutalaiba took leave of him and headed home, for she had other fish to fry, and didn't have time to waste on such paltry matters.

Makiera's family had forsaken her and turned their backs on her. With nothing to hang onto except some hazy memories that were likely to turn into meaningless visions and powerful motivations to act aggressively. The saddest moments were when she could remember she had children, but not one of them took the trouble to come over to see her.

Sometimes, she had a pathetic voice inside her that kept telling her that she deserved all the bad things that were happening to her. She spent the next few months all by herself; she spent every minute alone in her room, refusing to associate with or be in the company of her inmates. She would stare at the floor for hours on end, rebuffing any invitation from any psychiatric nurse to take her for a walk down the mental health facility garden. The following week, and after having learned about his mother's loss of memory through the agency of his aunt, Sadij decided to drop in on his mother. To his great surprise, Makiera didn't recognise him, but when he tried to identify himself as being her elder son, she sent him away with a flea in the air.

'In your dreams! My son, Sadij, is still a little boy! You big fat fibber. Get along with you! And don't expect me to believe what you're saying!'

To prompt her memory, Sadij brought some photos of one of his birthdays where they were together. He then kept a picture on display featuring his late grandmother, Moukafiha, and commented,

'That lady dressed in white that you see on the right is your late mother and my grandmother, may her soul rest peace, Mrs Moukafiha.'

That was more than Mrs Makiera could bear because, to her, her mother was still alive. Out of fury and with a sudden and unexpected movement, she quickly snatched the picture frame out of her son's hand and flung it onto the floor, yelling out some swear words at Sadij, *'Shut the fuck up, bastard! You think I'm nuts?'*

The nurse who was administering some medication to another patient in the adjoining room heard the sound of the breaking glass front that was used to protect the picture as it came smashing down the floor, filling the room with its fragments. The nurse came in and asked Sadij to wait outside. She then injected her with a very powerful sedative, while two other nurses were holding her hands. A few seconds later came the psychiatrist to make sure everything was all right. Whereupon, Sadij explained to him what came to pass. The therapist reassured Sadij that loss of memory was one of the symptoms associated with dementia and that his mother was likely to travel back in time.

'As I told your aunt last time, there's more likelihood that your mother will stop recognising you. You have to be very patient. All you need to do is to avoid trying to bring her to reason 'cause this will undoubtedly piss her off. Instead, try to enter her world and play her game. Right?'

Sadij nodded his head in approval, took leave of the doctor and went away.

Chapter 12

That evening, Sadij went into his flat feeling a deep void in his heart; that most intense wish of finding his mother getting better had abated, giving way to a lugubrious look that had recently taken hold of his face. He decided to stay at home for the whole week, unwilling to venture out and encounter any other dismal occurrence that was likely to make his frail life harder and more tenuous. He no longer wanted to meet new girls because he became convinced that he had nothing to offer them except permanent annoyance and bother. Worse than that, he was utterly convinced that any nymph he was going to date would end up leaving him.

The trauma he had experienced for years after his mother's divorce, her remarriage and his recent failed attempts at finding his soul mate had contributed to his current state of insecurity. The double whammy of being rejected by his mother and at the same time exploited by his partners triggered negative thoughts about himself and those around him. Again, and to assuage his sorrow, he decided to get out and engage with life. To that end, he reached out to his alter ego, Jaaba, for entertainment and consolation; they both threw parties and lived it up.

On one of those pleasurable social gatherings, he was introduced by his close friend to a very beautiful French girl named Elodie. She was small in stature while her build was athletic; the young lady looked like Venus, for she had a rocking body and a very cute face. She was agile, supple, lively; she had a flat forehead, a small Greek nose and green almond-shaped eyes. Her gaze was brilliant and sparkling; her lips were thin and, whenever she smiled, she had the knack of drawing an enticing dimple on her chin. No one could escape noticing her puffy and pinkish cheeks. She had platinum blonde hair that was reduced of its brightness into an ashy colour. All the guys that were present at the party were fascinated by her looks and personality, and Sadij was no exception. She seemed to be true and enjoyed the simple pleasures of life with no fuss.

Sadij quickly fell in love with her and tried to get closer to her; however, working up the courage to talk to her turned out to be a very daunting and terrifying challenge. He sparked up a conversation with her, hoping to ask her out. *'Jaaba has told me so much about you,'* he said, looking a bit embarrassed.

Elodie chuckled and said, *'Really? What did he tell you?'*

Sadij tried to make the whole thing up in the hope of winning a date; he, therefore, replied, *'Just nice and good things, and I've been looking forward to seeing you.'*

Elodie looked relaxed and was as customary in a joyful mood. She kept laughing and sending signals to Sadij that she was interested in him too. She immediately created an instant connection with her beautiful eyes. This imbued Sadij with a sense of trust that made him more willing to engage with her. He couldn't believe that he was there talking to a very cute girl, who was the centre of attention of all guys present at the party. He knew he couldn't make her fall in love with him; nevertheless, he could at least increase his chances of finally having a happy love affair and winning the heart of the woman he had been longing for.

He then asked her for a favour, *'Could you please hold my jacket while I fetch some drinks for us?'* Elodie grabbed the jacket and smiled again.

When Sadij returned with the drinks, he asked her, *'I guess you're very familiar with this place... I mean the fourteenth district of Paris. Aren't you?'*

She answered looking a bit surprised, *'Yeah. Why are you asking?'*

He reassured her, saying, *'Well, I just would like to know if there's any good place to eat around here.'*

She wasn't the kind of girl that was reared to be wary of guys she didn't know. She immediately answered his question in a very funny manner, *'If I have heard you correctly, you're asking me out on a date.'*

Sadij felt more and more comfortable and took things up a notch, *'To be honest, I would be more than happy to invite you out.'*

While Sadij was speaking, Elodie's brain was reading and analysing the way he was holding his body and every move he was making.

She then said with her usual sparkling smile, *'Don't you think that you're getting a little bit ahead of yourself?'*

Sadij showed that he was harmless and tried to make Elodie feel at ease. *'I just thought that it would be a great opportunity to get to know each other.'*

Seeing that Sadij was determined to make her acquaintance, she accepted the invitation.

Chapter 13

For the first time, Sadij felt uncomfortable eating in front of a woman, and Elodie was not just like any other woman. She was wearing a very tight-fitting dress that hugged her figure and accentuated her physical assets. That sexy dress showed her big boobs out of her dress, and the high-heeled shoes she was wearing foregrounded her beautiful legs. Almost all customers who were having dinner that night kept looking at her. Sadij was embarrassed being in the company of a very pretty lady that took delight in dressing herself revealingly. So, he kept writhing in his seat, looking around to see if Elodie was being viewed sexually by any men around. She was a woman that no one could help noticing and not forgetting. Sadij tried his utmost to not come across as preachy. When the waiter came to take orders, she smiled at him and asked him in a way that suggested she didn't want him to take her seriously.

'If I were your intimate girlfriend, what would you recommend me to eat?'

The waiter stood speechless for a moment, cast a furtive glance at Elodie's partner, noticed that the latter was blushing at Elodie's unexpected audacity and replied, *'Well, it depends on each person's taste. But if I was to bring my girlfriend here one day, I would advise her to order a palatable and delicious steak tartare.'*

Elodie smiled and winked at the waiter, who construed this flirtatious signal as admiration and appreciation. Sadij didn't seem to appreciate Elodie's provocative behaviour much. He knew in his own heart of hearts that she was a mysterious and seductive lady whose charm and physical assets were bound to ensnare any man that happened to run into her in fetters of irresistible desire. From the first meeting at that party, Sadij was seduced and kind of hypnotised by that devourer of males that was Elodie. She had managed to make him fall to his knees at her feet. During that night's dinner, Sadij learned that Elodie had already a boyfriend that loved her to death and that she got along with.

However, she admitted that she didn't know what she felt about him. She also admitted to having several relationships that had fallen through for reasons that she didn't wish to unravel. Sadij was just listening to what she was relating, and it was only when she informed him that her family along with that of her lover were leaving together on vacation for three weeks that he was completely disheartened. He suggested an outing, but she declined the invitation under the pretext that she was very busy at the moment.

Chapter 14

The vampirish love that Elodie stood for started sucking the life out of Sadij and driving him to his devastation. The poor chap was lovesick; he could neither eat nor sleep. He realised that he was falling in love with her; she kept popping into his head, against his own will. Now, he was wondering where she could be, was she alone, or with somebody else? Was she thinking of him as much as he was thinking about her? All of a sudden, a crazy idea occurred to him; *How about calling her?*

He was on the point of doing so were it not for his apprehension of the fact that he might appear overeager and kind of pushy. In an attempt to get her out of his mind, if only for a few minutes, he decided to go for a walk. While strolling along the Champs-Elysées Avenue, he caught sight of a jewellery store and went in. Once inside, he remembered seeing Elodie wearing that sexy dress with a peacock brooch attached to it. Most enticing of all was that golden ankle bracelet she was wearing on the left ankle. She was so put together that all the guys that were present at the party believed she was a princess. He knew that she was too much to handle and satisfy and that with the salary that he earned, he could only afford to offer her a golden ring that would cost him around one thousand francs. He – without any further hesitation – bought it and called her up, saying that there was something really important he would like to tell her.

A few minutes later, Elodie showed up, wearing a very tight, red, low-cut neckline dress meant to show the goods on purpose, black leather pointed-toe heeled pumps, with a leather black handbag in her hand. She was a woman who cared so much about her appearance.

When Sadij saw her, he thought that she was just out of his league and that he had better not try with her. He kept saying to himself, *'She's too good for me. What if she turns down my gift and shoots me down? How am I going to save face if that happens?'*

She immediately launched the conversation, asking, *'What's that thing that's so important that you want to talk to me about?'*

Her question caught him completely off guard; he felt confused and uncertain as to how to go about acknowledging his love to her.

'This isn't the right place to talk about it. So, let's go to that café,' said Sadij pointing to a French brasserie that was close by.

Elodie seemed to be in a great hurry. *'Honestly, I don't have time to breathe. Let's get this over with. Shall we?'*

Sadij replied, *'I assure you that it won't be too long. Trust me.'*

She agreed and they both went into the brasserie. As soon as they got in, a guy that was sitting at the counter exclaimed, *'Wow! She is so beautiful.'*

Elodie was more aesthetically appealing and sexually attractive to look at. As soon as they sat at the table, Sadij took a ring wrapped in a red tiny box out of his pocket. When Elodie saw the red tiny box, she reacted joyfully with wide eyes and a radiant smile, saying in a very soft and hardly audible voice, *'Oh, dear one, you oughtn't to have taken the trouble to do this. Thank you.'*

Sadij was reassured and he said, *'Please accept this ring as a promise that I will be the best boyfriend that you'll ever—'*

Before he had time to express his feelings, Elodie's mobile rang. She took her phone out of her handbag, cast a glance at it, blushed and evinced some uneasiness. She tried not to betray herself, kissed Sadij on the cheek and departed, leaving him motionless.

How soft her lips were! And how peculiarly her kiss invaded all his senses!

Chapter 15

Sadij couldn't get Elodie off his mind. Even during the busiest moments at his work where he was busy keeping audits and inspecting the financial records of some firms, he found himself thinking about her, wishing from the bottom of his heart that he could share every single thing with her. How odd this was, for he couldn't explain how she had managed to occupy a never-ending space in both his mind and his heart. All his thoughts were being obsessed with this femme fatale. He couldn't figure out what was happening to him.

While reclining his head on the pillow, he started musing, *Am I getting infatuated with her? Or am I crazy loving her? Am I growing attracted to her physically or emotionally?*

Sadij was unable to rationally explain the kind of attraction that he had for her. He then reverted to self-reflection again. *'Why am I attracted to her? What is the special thing about her that appealed to me?'* He found out no cogent answers to his questions. Soon afterward, he called her up asking if she would like to have dinner with him; she told him that she didn't have time.

He then said, *'How about having lunch together tomorrow?'*

She said, *'I don't have time.'*

He asked her, *'When is your next day off?'*

She said, *'I'm snowed under every day. I'll call you back*

when I'm free. Listen, Sadij, I have to go now. Something has just come up.'

Before his phone conversation ended, Sadij had heard a male voice calling Elodie. He became increasingly confused and puzzled, for if she were interested in his invitation, she might have said we could try another day. *What if she is dating another guy? Who's that guy that was calling her?*

Elodie grew up into a poor family of seven children that lived in the suburbs of Angoulême in the South-West of France. She dropped out of school at the age of sixteen; and since there was no visible prospect of success for an ambitious young girl in that backward area, Elodie decided – against her father's will – to head for Paris, the city of light. Once on-site, she worked as a waitress in a brasserie near Montparnasse and rented a maid's room in Belleville's District. It was in that Montparnasse Brasserie that a guy spotted her and advised her to get in touch with the management of Moulin Rouge Cabaret, as they were hiring. And as a very charming young lady, Elodie knew quite well how to put her sexy looks to good use. Her work consisted in getting guys, through the use of her voluptuous body and seductive tactics, to buy very expensive alcoholic drinks. As a bottle server, she earned a fixed monthly wage and commissions based on the number of bottles sold. To be able to afford a sumptuous outfit she was extremely fond of, she worked overtime as a Moulin Rouge dancer on weekends. Her sexually alluring figure earned her many well-to-do admirers at that famous French cabaret institution. She was very pretty to look at, and didn't mind letting men enjoy her dancing and her incredible body. In addition to her night job, she would from time to time accept an old rich man's invitation to dine out in return for money. And that was how she had made acquaintance with a fat cat working in Matignon. That dude had bought her a cosy flat in a residential area near La Defense. He did furnish and redecorate the apartment to Elodie's liking. Each time that rich man met her in that apartment, he gave her five thousand francs, and if she needed any more money while he wasn't around, he would transfer her as much as she wanted.

One sunny morning, while Elodie was lounging on a feather-stuffed settee convertible click-clack, softly stroking a glass of champagne with her beautifully manicured fingertips, her mobile started ringing. It was Sadij calling again! She refused to answer his call, but he kept on calling. She found it neither cute nor endearing of him to call her all the time; this really got on her nerves. As she didn't wish to speak to him, she rejected his calls. Sadij got so carried away by the dazzling excitement of his new love experience that he didn't predict that things could turn sour one day. Elodie started getting worried sick because she found the needy behaviour of Sadij utterly off-putting.

However, Sadij, blinded by love, was craving to know why she refused to answer his calls so he, therefore, texted her, saying, *"I'm getting worried. I hope you're doing pretty fine. Please, reassure me that everything is okay with you."*

Elodie started losing interest in having Sadij as a boyfriend, for she realised that he posed a threat to her material comfort and privacy. To that end, she tried her utmost to avoid him. But Sadij went so far as to keep close tabs on her; he got into the habit of stalking her, keeping track of every move she made, without her knowledge. He even used the PanSpy mobile tracking software to track her location. One night, that clingy behaviour had led him to land at a restaurant where she was having dinner with the old rich man that provided for her. It dawned upon him that she was seeing someone else, and was doing it for money. He was consumed with jealousy.

He subconsciously started comparing himself with the man who was dating his girlfriend. *Am I less attractive than him? What does that guy have that I don't? What has she got to do with a poor guy like me?*

Sadij felt threatened and started seeing all his chances of winning Elodie's heart reduced to nothing. He felt anger and anxiety rising inside him, and was in a quandary about what to do. Just outside the restaurant's doors, he stood glaring at them. The man seemed to be friendly, and Elodie was smiling and elatedly chatting with him; Sadij started imagining and projecting things on their interactions. After they had finished their dinner, they didn't hang around, for the old man gave her a ride over to her flat in his Porsche. Sadij drove closely behind them to watch them. After a few minutes, the couple got to their destination. By pushing a single button, the guy opened the garage door of the building with a remote-control garage opener and down went the car.

Part V

Chapter 1

Sadij couldn't shake the premonition that Elodie was just using him, and taking advantage of his generosity; she knew that he had a soft spot for her and she accordingly used his kindness to buy her a sumptuous new pair of shoes and some stylish handbags to keep up with the latest fashion trends. What irritated Sadij was that Elodie offered nothing in return except for empty words and lies. The tell-tale sign that showed Sadij that Elodie was a materialistic girl was when she needed money, she would call him.

But as soon as she got what she wanted, she would ignore him for a week or two. Every time she disregarded him and snubbed him, he found himself falling more and more madly in love with her. She was playing him like a puppet. And the fact that she was spending less and less time with him meant that there was another guy in her life; but the saddest thing in all of that was that only God knew what she was doing that night with an old man that didn't love her even half as much as Sadij did. So, he was just like a scapegoat filling up the blanks when her rich "*amant*" wasn't available for her. Instead of taking the high ground and severing ties with her, he decided to bring the matter to a head by confronting her and speaking his piece to her face once and for all.

One morning, when she was about to go out shopping, he paid her an unannounced visit. As he didn't have the access code to the residence, he stayed glued to the lamppost that was next to the entrance of the building. The moment she drove her red Mini Austin car out of the garage, she found him standing in the driveway. He could have got run over by the car if Elodie hadn't braked in time.

Beside herself with ire, she got out of the car and started shouting at him, '*Have you gone stark raving mad? You scared the hell out of me. I could have killed you. Tell me, all this boils down to what?*'

Sadij encouraged her to not get agitated and relax. '*Would you get a grip on yourself? Please cool your jets.*'

'*How do you want me to calm down? You scared me to death,*' she said in a very shaky voice.

Sadij realised the magnitude of the blunder he had just committed and apologised. '*I honestly didn't mean it. You can't imagine how sorry I am. Is there anything I can do to make it up to you, dearest one? Please forgive me. I promise this won't happen again.*' He had no sooner got hold of her hand than she let out a sharp piercing cry.

'*Don't touch me! Leave me alone. Get out of my way! This is more than I can take.*'

'*I just want to talk to you,*' he said.

'*We have nothing more to say to each other. You had better go now,*' she strongly advised him.

Sadij was determined this time to have it out with her, '*I'm not here to shoot the breeze. I've come to talk to you about the two of us.*'

Elodie was getting nervous, and could no longer put up with his clingy behaviour. She finally laid it on the line.

'*Frankly speaking, your calling me most of the time gets on my nerves. I need some space. I need time to think, okay?*

For the time being, I just don't know what I want.'

Sadij looked sad and disappointed, for the young lady he was head over heels in love with was giving him the reality check that the fascination had always been one-sided.

He almost burst into tears, saying in a very pathetic voice, *'I thought you had the same feelings towards me. We've got along with each other for more than six months, and everything seemed just so fine, and now I can't help but notice all the big red flags.'*

Elodie noticed that Sadij's countenance was taking on a very gloomy expression, and she, therefore, tried to make him understand that he didn't have anything to do with that.

'It's not you, it's me, and I think we should have a break for a while.'

'You're going to ditch me only when hell freezes over,' he angrily reacted, violently hitting the hood of the car with his fist.

Elodie was extremely frightened by Sadij's aggressive behaviour. For the first time, she came to realise that she was in a relationship with a guy who had major temper issues. So, she availed herself of this alarming sign to put an end to being in a relationship with a man who was unable to manage his anger, and said in a very self-assured tone,

'Look, Sadij, I can't be with a man who loses his calm over really petty issues. When I first saw you, I thought you were a reasonable and thoughtful guy. But now, you're seriously starting to scare me. You need to consult a psychologist for anger management.'

All of a sudden, he realised that he nearly screwed things up, and made an apology. *'I don't know how that could have happened. Believe me, I didn't mean it that way. How can I*

243

make it up to you?'

At this moment, it dawned upon Elodie that if she continued to argue, she would inevitably provoke him to get into conflict, and this would not lighten up the situation; therefore, she kept herself calm and tried to talk peacefully.

'Forget about it, now. I'll let you off this time. Right? And now, I have to go shopping. Let's remain in touch. Shall we?'

They kissed goodbye and went their separate ways.

Chapter 2

Sadij started having a sinking feeling in the pit of his stomach that his relationship with Elodie was getting utterly confusing and frustrating because he felt that she was growing tired of him, and wasn't quite sure about what he meant to her. Sadij found it hard to focus on his work; every time he attempted to apply himself to his work, the idea that Elodie was trying to ditch him kept running through his mind.

'I just can't figure out how things were on point some months ago, and then now I feel like she wants nothing to do with me. Every time I ask her out, she says she's very busy; she's merely trying to avoid hanging out with me. Had she wanted to talk to me and spend more time with me, she would undoubtedly have worked hard to find a way to do so. Instead, she's just avoiding my calls and making up excuses so she can go out with someone else.'

To make sure whether Elodie was playing around behind his back, and to get clarity before wading any further through his doubts, Sadij decided to talk to her about it. This time, he had some tough questions he wanted to ask her. But every time he wanted to bring up the issue with her, she was reluctant to have an honest conversation with him. And this only gave rise to greater misgivings. Her refusal to have it out with him just made Sadij very nervous and susceptible to quarrel. He once again started harassing her by constantly calling her; and since she didn't want to answer his calls, he decided to contact her through emails and social media.

But when all those methods of contact had proved inefficient, he once more resorted to spying on her. It dawned upon him that Elodie was only trying to get rid of him; he felt like a victim being toyed with, and this fear of being abandoned by a lady he genuinely cherished in his innermost heart didn't allow him to reason any more.

'How dare she dump me like a piece of trash? I will never let that happen.'

So, Sadij had that repetitive thought pattern that kept playing inside his head just like a broken record. He became obsessed with her, stalking and following her wherever she went. One day, while she was having dinner with the same guy in a very sumptuous restaurant close to Montparnasse, Sadij started making up details in his head about a potentially sexual relationship between Elodie and that old rich guy; he was even sure of it now that the old man was holding Elodie's hand in his. To make sure where he stood in his relationship with Elodie, Sadij went up straight to the table where they were sitting.

Suddenly and without any warning, he shouted out, *'After all I have done for you... Why are you doing this to me? Don't you care about me?'*

Elodie looked neither embarrassed nor shocked; she, on the contrary, acted like she didn't know Sadij. The latter kept on guilting her and seeking her sympathy at the same time.

The rich man turned to Elodie and asked, *'Do you know him?'*

In a very reassuring voice, Elodie responded, *'Of course, I don't. I have never seen that man before; he must have me* confused with someone else.'

Upon hearing this, Sadij got more furious and started calling Elodie every name under the sun. *'I thought you had the same feelings towards me, but I was wrong; you were merely taking advantage of me. I was just a very stupid go-to guy and a man Friday you were using to further your selfish whims. Now, you say you don't know me. You ugly slut. You will regret it.'*

Elodie acted as if she had never met Sadij before in that she continued denying having anything to do with him. Elodie's rich *"amant"*, unable to put up with Sadij's disparaging slights, stood up and punched him in the face. Whereupon, Sadij fell flat on his face. A few seconds later, a security guard came and brutally yanked Sadij out of the restaurant. While the security officer was dragging Sadij out of the place, an avalanche of intimidating threats jarred on Elodie's nerves and ears.

Chapter 3

Disgusted and deeply disappointed, Sadij retreated into his shell and didn't speak to anyone for nearly a week. After being humiliated in public, he was so sad that he looked back ruefully and in anger on those moments when she was craving to eat something outside, or when she wanted him to buy her something precious, she would reach out to him. Whenever she condescended to go out with him for a cup of coffee and a chat, he had to pay for her. She took delight in having all the things that she wanted for free. She wouldn't miss out on any opportunities to use Sadij to her own advantage because he seemed to have it all together. How stupid of him to feel that there was a click and that they were bonding! It dawned upon him that Elodie was acting the same way to any prey that happened to come her way and catch her bait.

Much to his displeasure, he now realised that Elodie was not into guys who were tight with money, she rather preferred socialising and mingling with well-to-do men. Unlike him, an old rich man would provide her with everything she might need, and her life would be secure and filled with excitingly strange holidays and costly presents. In hindsight, Sadij was moved to tears because he became aware of the fact that he was merely a scapegoat that had been filling up the blanks all along when the other guy wasn't available. Now, he bore a huge grudge against her, and those tender feelings that he had hitherto harboured for her turned into malicious spite and venomous ill will; all his dreams that included Elodie and that he'd been strenuously weaving fizzled out within a fraction of a second.

He tried hard to suppress his anger while sitting at the table in the kitchen; but he eventually succumbed to that burning ire that was smouldering in his gut, thus thrusting with all his might a nearby knife into that wooden kitchenette table. Instead of moving on with his life and turning over a new leaf, he dwelt on his sorrow and remained lugubrious. He felt slighted and became less forgiving and less benevolent. He tried to trivialise the humiliation he had gone through, but to no avail, for the anger's flames that were stoked by his vengeful feelings lay in his ruminations. To escape from the trauma that he had experienced at the hands of Elodie, he reached out to a local bar that was quite close by.

He slowly trudged to a pub-like neighbourhood hangout for trendy singles that was located in boulevard St Michel. There was a romantic mood that hung over that place, with candles sitting on every table and a piece of soft and unobtrusive music being played on a jukebox. He sat on a barstool next to two chaps and ordered a beer. The conversation in which the two guys were engaged grabbed his attention; so he eavesdropped on the exchange that was going on between the two guys, drank his first beer and ordered this time draft beer.

'Alas! Nice and selfless girls are getting scarce nowadays, my pal. All you have is rapacious and greedy bitches,' said one of the two guys.

Upon hearing this, Sadij decided to buy rounds, fed liquor to the two guys and enthusiastically engaged in the discussion.

'I agree with you, man. The only thing that matters to those sluts is money. They're adepts at extracting money from us guys.'

The guy, who was sitting next to Sadij, expressed his disagreement. *'To be honest, I have never been caught in their web. I can see through all their wicked wiles. I've been dating whores for a long time, and I know what they're up to. They enjoy all the frills and perks that come to them from silly guys that work very hard to provide for their wanton and insatiable needs.'* The great amount of alcohol that Sadij had swallowed made him weird, and his mind was immediately taken to the last scuffle he had had with Elodie and her *"amant"*.

His body felt warm and he felt like the two guys at the counter were his best friends, and was yearning to tell them about his love story with Elodie, and how he was trifled with. So, he started talking about how he was so in love with Elodie that he couldn't let go of her… *'And lately I found out that she had been cheating on me with an old smurf.'* He stopped and out of spite threw his liquor on the floor.

The bartender got furious and asked Sadij, *'Come on, man! What the hell are you doing?'*

When Sadij heard one of his favourite songs played, he stood, and hit the dance floor, and reiterated the lyrics of "Easy Lover", while sipping the remaining drops of liquor left in his glass. He then walked to the bar and asked the bartender to serve him another beer, which the young man at the counter immediately declined. He requested a drink a second time, but the bartender explained that his manager had told him not to serve him. Sadij felt highly offended, humiliated and embarrassed, especially when that humiliation occurred in the presence of his two new best friends that witnessed the situation. So, as he was giddy, he got wild, reckless and started calling the bartender and his manager names. The manager realised that Sadij was in the grip of alcohol; he, therefore, beckoned to a bouncer and told him to expel Sadij from the bar.

Instead of going straight home, he decided to walk to Elodie's flat in that wild and boozy condition. He felt rejected, helpless, powerless and very weak in the wake of his realisation that his love for Elodie was not reciprocated; to him, the world now seemed to be a very cold and ugly place and he wished he had never been born. When he got to the place, he couldn't have access to the building because it was equipped with a security code. Therefore, he had to wait for some time till an inhabitant of the building showed up. At last, he managed to enter the building. He rang the bell several times; Elodie, who wasn't expecting anyone to come at this time of the day, peered through the peephole to make sure who the caller was before opening. To her astonishment, she saw Sadij right there standing at the door. He knew that she was in and didn't want to open the door.

He slurred and stammered, *'I know you're in… just… want… to talk to you. Open the door.'*

'There isn't anything more we can say to each other. If you don't go away, I will call the police,' she said in a threatening voice.

'Go ahead and call them. You don't scare me. Open that fucking door, or I'll break it down.'

The stubbornness with which he persisted in asking her to open the door for him compelled her to call the police. A few minutes later, the police forces came, arrested Sadij and took him to the police station where he was placed in custody, as

251

Elodie had filed a complaint as a result of her being incessantly harassed by him. On the premises of the police station, Sadij was taken to task for having molested Elodie, and was obliged to stay overnight in a police cell. The morning after, and before he was released, he had been ordered to sign a recognisance to swear he will not annoy Elodie any longer.

Chapter 4

Sadij's fear of losing loved ones started when he was very young, especially when he had experienced that traumatic absence of his father in his life. From that moment onward, he began to fear losing other important persons in his life. That fear of abandonment did have a significant effect upon his life and all the failed relationships he had had. He had always wanted to have that continual reassurance that any girl he was emotionally attached to loved him and would stay with him, and that was why he had always sought to please all the girls he had known, giving too much in his relationships.

Unfortunately, he wasn't able to maintain any relationship, and things just didn't work out as he had expected. That bright, bubbly and ambitious young Sadij was gone; that funny Sadij that used to crack jokes was dead now. He locked himself up in his room for nearly three days, refusing to talk to anyone and distancing himself from others. He closed all the shutters of his apartment and stayed in the dark. He felt he should take his own life, as he didn't have self-confidence. He felt he wasn't welcome in this world.

He even didn't want anything any more; nothing mattered to him now, because he felt hopeless. He could no longer mingle with people because he felt that they would take advantage of him, which he wouldn't be able to put up with; he felt that making friends or getting to know new girls might anchor him to them, and it would be very hard for him to survive their wilful and unexpected abandonment of him. Now, more than ever, he felt that the easiest and safest course of action was to remain by himself, apart and detached. He spent most of his time in a room that was cluttered with knick-knacks; his flat was spilling over with old newspapers, plastic containers and books. He had lived in utter filth for almost two weeks now, with rotten food in his fridge, rotten junk food in the sink and a toilet filled to the brim with dirt. Amid this disorderly world and squalor, he devoted most of his time to bemoaning his lot. He was so depressed and hopeless that he didn't have the energy to straighten up his room. The desk at which he used to sit arranging the files of the company he worked for was a jumbled mess strewn with papers and envelopes. Careless about his physical appearance, his hair became wild and unkempt; he had also allowed his beard to grow out of proportion.

He felt he had reached a point of no return and was sort of losing hope and control; depression got a grip on him, making him feel like his soul had been sucked out and the few remaining vestiges of happiness and hope that were left within him were squeezed out. He spent time reliving and reconstructing in his mind's eye all those sad and painful moments that he had experienced in his life, thus embroiling himself in the dark depths of despair.

Chapter 5

When he woke up one morning, he caught a glimpse of a streak of light that peeped through a small aperture in the front door of the flat and decided not to yield to the urge to live in the past. He finally realised that feeling sorry for himself and blaming others wouldn't get him on the right side of feeling better. So, he resolved that he needed – now more than ever before – to get his life back on track. He felt that it was high time he rolled up his sleeves to get his life together. To begin with, he took out of the fridge some stinking rotten food that had started giving off a very unpleasant smell, washed an endless pile of dirty dishes that had been sitting in the sink for some weeks now, cleaned the toilet that was filled to the brim with toilet paper, shit and piss and picked up the plastic refuse bags that were scattered all over the kitchenette. When he opened the door to take the trash out, he bumped into his neighbour, Mrs Chailloux; the old lady was taken aback by Sadij's queer and shabby outward appearance. As soon as her eyes met his, she dashed for her flat and slammed the door. Sadij felt appalled by the insinuation of her act; he was bummed out that she had never taken the trouble to get to know him, just like the rest of the Parisians.

Mrs Chailloux's behaviour had made Sadij feel judged, mistreated and discriminated against. It was hard for a guy, who was about to make a fresh start, not to feel hurt and angry.

This negative and misplaced reaction of hers did damage Sadij's frail emotional health and became a real impediment to his prospective goals. The same anguish bubbled up when he went to work and was fired by the management for having failed to notify them of his unjustified absence. Jobless and broke, Sadij was now running the risk of getting evicted by his landlady.

He, therefore, went to a nearby stall where newspapers were sold, bought a local paper that occasionally posted job offers, and made his way toward the Luxembourg Gardens to peruse – at his leisure – all the job offers listed in the paper. Unfortunately, he failed to land all the jobs that he had interviewed for because of his looks. Ostracised, Sadij held a bitter grudge against the French society. To secure some help, he joined an association representing Muslims in France (The Union of Islamic Organisations of France (UIOF). Within that religious circle that was looked on with dubiousness by the French authorities, Sadij made friends with some religious hardliners, who immediately accepted to put him up and took him on as an editorial assistant for their newly created magazine.

Only yesterday, Sadij was feeling alienated and rejected, because he was fired and was running the risk of getting evicted from his abode. Now, all his worries and troubles seemed to have disappeared, thanks to those altruistic Muslim brothers that had given him that which the French society and even his own family had failed to do; namely security, recognition and, above all, an identity. He now felt he belonged and his life did, at last, make some sense. On one of those famous meetings that were held once a week by the association, Tarik, a very charismatic radical preacher, was delivering his acerbic tirade against the French government.

'All the problems that our young third-generation suffer from are prompted by the unfair policy of exclusion and marginalisation carried out by the French government. The future of our children in this country remains uncertain, for they have no access to the labour market. The ungratefulness of the French government is so blatant that it has paid lip-service to the promises made about the integration of our children; their malignant agenda resides in distorting and skewing the minds of our children; they only want to instil pernicious ideas into the minds of our children, and lead them astray. Let's remain on our guard! They're waging a war against Islam. Let's come together and nip their wicked plans in the bud! We're living in a nation of unbelievers and miscreants. It's our religious duty to fight them, and do our utmost to make the Islamic law prevail in this country.'

While this bigoted preacher was sermonising, Sadij was listening with rapt attention, imbibing the gist of the preacher's message. By dint of attending these regular religious gatherings, Sadij ended up being receptive to the pernicious and venomous messages of religious radicals. Now, he firmly believed that to redress the grievances he had been nursing against all the people that had wronged him, he should kind of resort to violence. So, he started thinking about how to avenge himself against his alleged enemies. The first person that popped into his head was Elodie.

A few hours after leaving an abandoned warehouse at the corner of rue du Bois, St Louis, where the gatherings took place, Sadij went straight home, took some of his stuff therefrom, went out and took the RER towards La Défense. He wasn't born a criminal but was made one, for at no time in his life did he have an intrinsic propensity for cruelty. But because of the ordeals he had been through and the pernicious impact of the religious indoctrination he had been exposed to, he became just like a living ticking bomb waiting to go off at any time. He was only waiting for the right moment to discharge that overwhelming and insatiable anger that had long been seething within him.

At the entrance to the building, Sadij was waiting and anticipating the opening of the building's garage. To avoid being recognised, he was wearing a disguise of glasses, a fake moustache, and a cap. A few minutes later, a man pulled up in his red sports car in front of the driveway that led up to the building and opened the garage with magnetic card access. While the guy was driving his car into the underground parking lot, Sadij swiftly followed behind him quietly and stealthily. He hid behind a concrete pillar located near the door of the parking area that led to the elevator and lay in ambush, waiting for Elodie to return home. He knew at what time she would finish her work.

At around midnight, a red Mini Austin car entered the garage, and in it was the poor blonde lady. As soon as Elodie pulled the car up at her own parking space and got out of the car, Sadij approached her from behind, brandished a knife he took out of his pocket, instructed her to keep quiet and demanded her to go up to her flat in a very discreet manner and without arousing suspicion.

Elodie was shuddering with fear, and the only thing she was thinking about was how to save her skin. She begged Sadij not to hurt her and promised she would do whatever he asked her.

Once inside, Sadij gagged her and tied her to a chair in her bedroom where he started torturing her physically and psychologically. She couldn't fight for herself because she was just like a bird with broken wings. Her legs and hands were immobilised.

Sadij put the knife to Elodie's throat and began sliding it smoothly over the skin of her face, saying, *'You're very proud of your physical beauty. And you do care so much about your appearance, you selfish slut. I guess you fear looking ugly; but what if I blemish your face and leave a lingering injury that will mar the perfection of your selfish face? Eh? So what do you think?'*

Elodie couldn't talk and was just writhing in her chair.

Sadij then continued his speech, *'You think you can get away with it just like that? I loved you, you filthy whore. I bought you the most expensive clothes so that you can keep up with the latest fashion trends, worked very hard to buy you costly jewels that most whores like you are raving about. But all you care about is money and attracting idiots like me.'* He had no sooner finished this last statement than he slapped her face and tore her red tight dress off with the knife.

He proceeded with his sharp and corrosive rebuke, *'It doesn't matter to you if a poor guy like me pays your bills; you dirty slut… you enjoy having things for free. Don't you? You've used and abused me to your advantage. You despise guys who are tight with money like me, that's why you love mingling with rich guys, just like that Papa Smurf of yours. You said you don't know me, and you allowed that jerk to punch me in the face and in public. Eh? How do you feel being at my mercy? I will impair that face of yours and you will never be able to hang out and get into that stinky rich people's inner circle. I thought you loved me, but I was wrong. The only thing you care about is money and yourself, of course. Whenever I offer you a gift, you touch my hands or hold my arms, making me believe you're doing it spontaneously. But you were only trifling with my feelings.'*

Sadij got so infuriated that he sliced Elodie's cheek with the tip of the knife, causing a long slash from her cheek to her chin. In no time, Elodie's bosom was covered with blood. At the sight of her blood, she fainted. A few minutes later when she came to, she felt a whirling sensation; it was as if everything around her was rotating and spinning.

Meanwhile, Sadij went to the bathroom where there was a medicine cabinet, brought an antiseptic spray, applied it at the site of the cut to stop the blood flow that was now trickling onto the floor. He then took her mobile and checked her messages. When he came across a message sent by her rich *amant*, informing her that he would be seeing her during the weekend, Sadij replied, on behalf of Elodie, that she wouldn't be free, for she would be staying with her family and that she would call him back as soon as she got back home. Afterward, he turned Elodie's phone off, blindfolded her, and left the flat in the guise of a plumber.

Chapter 6

Elodie was really hungry and thirsty, for she had had nothing to eat and drink; her lips got parched and hunger started growling in her little stomach. She attempted to get up, wiggling her feet and hands and fidgeting in her chair; she now had spent two days lying prone as she had attempted to get up. Because of prolonged hunger, she felt dizzy, lightheaded and passed out. When she came round, she tried to open her eyes but couldn't. Her heart was beating so fast, and her pounding headache only intensified. She was sightless, stock-still, subdued and as dead as an autumn leaf. Before breathing her last, she, with great difficulty, tried to hang on to life, comforting herself that it was all a dream, all this wasn't real, and she would soon wake up; she attempted to free her tied arms by twisting, turning and pulling, but the narrow straps that were folded about her whole body kept digging into her skin. How she wished she could cry out for help and invite someone to her rescue, but in vain, for she was gagged. The more she tried to wrench her hands free, the deeper the straps sawed her frail flesh, drawing more and more blood. And in a hopeless and last-ditch effort, she hit the floor again and again with the back of her head. She struggled for breath with her mouth covered; however, pitch blackness continued to swallow her up. She felt her eyes close slowly, and finally surrendered herself to the darkness. Her body suddenly went limp.

It was half-past nine in the morning when the cleaning lady, who was employed by Elodie to do housework once a week, found her employer's body in the bedroom. She was so horrified at the sight of Elodie's body covered in blood that she uttered a long loud piercing cry that reverberated through the whole building. Elodie was the prettiest 'crazy horse danseuse' of the famous cabaret Moulin Rouge. Now, her arms were motionless, inanimate; she had dark purple bruises on her legs and arms. Her scarred face hung dangling down from the chair. The cleaning lady approached the corpse, took her pulse at the wrist and realised that Elodie was indeed dead. It was a shocking and emotionally draining experience for that maid. She had no idea what to do! She felt disoriented; it was as if her brain hadn't caught up to what her eyes had seen. A few minutes later, she realised that she had to report her employer's dead body and eventually called the police.

Soon, the cops were rushing through the front door and into the bedroom where Elodie lay without breath, without a pulse, all covered in blood. A police officer took the cleaning lady aside and started peppering her with questions. Another forensic scientist was collecting evidence, including fingerprints and bodily fluids at the crime scene. Sadij was on the suspect list following a one-time complaint that Elodie had filed against him. An alert was quickly issued by the police forces to arrest the main suspect. Meanwhile, Sadij was getting ready to leave the country for Afghanistan on a mission that was assigned to him by the head of the religious association, of which he had become a fervent and active member. He arrived three hours before his departure time. He went straight to the airline desk to check in; once he had his passport scanned, he received his boarding pass, and since he had only a carry-on small bag and no luggage to weigh, he got through the security screening. He was then asked to place his bag, his belt and any metal items he had on him in a white plastic tray.

At the customs and border protection, a border protection officer asked him, *'What's the purpose of your visit, sir?'*

Sadij felt a little bit intimidated, and it took him a while to respond, *'I'm traveling to explore the city of Kabul.'*

The border protection officer cast a dubious glance at Sadij, and asked him, *'How long will you be staying there?'*

Sadij was taken aback by this question, for he didn't see it coming and didn't seem to have the exact number of days he would be staying there; this embarrassing question did throw him off guard. While the customs officer was waiting for Sadij to answer his question, he received a call from one of his colleagues, telling him to arrest Sadij as a potential suspect in a murder case. He was immediately arrested by the police, transferred to the Paris police headquarters where he was kept in custody.

In the evening, and in an interrogation room, a police officer started grilling Sadij.

'Where were you on the fifth of December, from nine p.m. to midnight?'

'I was by myself. I mean in my room,' answered Sadij, who was shuddering with fear.

The police officer now got to the heart of the matter. *'Do you know a lady named Elodie?'*

Upon hearing her name, Sadij knew that he had really screwed up this time. He tried to steady his breath and dissemble his conspicuous panic. Fear crept over him like some ferocious and ravenous beast, paralysing his brain; it sucked the very breath and words from his mouth. How he wished he would run away from this confined space, but his feet wouldn't allow him to do so, and even if they did, he couldn't.

He eventually managed to open his mouth and said in a hardly audible voice, *'Yes, I do know her.'*

'When did you last see her?' asked the police officer.

'Well... we haven't seen each other since we broke up,' he answered in a very shaky voice. Sweat was dripping down from his forehead.

At last, the police officer disclosed what Sadij had feared most. *'We found her dead... I mean murdered in her flat. And it turns out that the DNA sample you gave us matches the fingerprints found at the crime scene. We have reasonable grounds to believe that you are the killer.'*

A sudden, overpowering feeling of fear washed over Sadij, the colour drained from his face, the fine hairs rose on the back of his neck and his mouth ran dry. He tried to open his mouth to speak, but words didn't come easy.

He put both hands on his head, broke down in tears, and confessed to the crime. *'I killed her because I loved her very much. Besides... she left me with no choice.'*

The police officer immediately rejected Sadij's claim of murdering Elodie out of love, saying, *'One never kills a woman one loves. You have to tell us what were the motives that had led you to kill Miss Elodie. You have to tell us the whole truth. Right?'*

Sadij couldn't find the right words to explain what happened; so, he ended up going off on a tangent, and the police officer couldn't understand what his true motives were.

Chapter 7

During a police search that was undertaken in the attic where Sadij had been taking up residence, the officers seized a blood-stained shirt, a computer, a hard disk, some documents belonging to the religious association and above all the knife Sadij had used to torture the late Elodie. Sadij was rapidly brought to justice charged with intentional and premeditated murder and subsequently sentenced to long-term imprisonment. In that very confined space, he became acutely aware of himself. At no time in his entire life had he ever imagined his body would be incarcerated; worse of all, his perception of time had been altered as well. Every day was pretty much like the day before. He had never imagined that he would find himself in a space that wasn't his; he had never fancied himself having no choice over who to be with and what meal to take. With threat and suspicion looming over, he grew more and more panicked. He was compelled to wear a permanent mask of impregnability to avoid being put upon by other inmates.

When he'd laid in bed suffering the effects of loneliness and isolation, all the dreams that he used to cherish in his innermost heart had suddenly resurfaced, bringing with them bitterness and regret. All the things that he had wanted and desired, things he'd clung on to and pinned all hopes on, had, in a wink of an eye, and in a bout of madness, fallen apart. All he was left with now was loss and grief.

He started reproaching himself, feeling guilty, *'Serves me right, for I acted like a jerk.'*

Disrupted and fragmented, and having virtually no family visiting to emotionally support him, Sadij was sullen and lugubrious; however, one day, his Aunt Moutalaiba dropped in to announce the death of his mother, Makiera. The latter took her own life in the lunatic asylum, leaving a note that said, *"I just wanna be happy."*

The End

CPSIA information can be obtained
at www.ICGtesting.com
Printed in the USA
BVHW031211240123
656976BV00004B/59

9 781800 742970